GOD WAITS OUTSIDE

A TRUE STORY
Caught in the Turkish and Greek Prison Systems,
A Labyrinth of Corruption and Lost Souls Forgotten

CAPTAIN MICHAEL CHURCHWARD

Print ISBN: 978-1-7348915-8-4
ebook ISBN: 978-1-7348915-7-7

Dedication

My Mother Elizabeth
My Brother Richard
We miss you both every day.

In memory of our beloved cousin, Leslie. We love you.

Special thanks to:
My brother Joe
My brother Tom
My brother Larry
My twin sister Michelle
My sister Doris
My sister Mary Kay
All my nieces and nephews
Nothing is more important than family.

The two Dianes' in my life:
My sister-in-law Diane
My dear friend Diane
Their friendship and caring without any conditions helped me get
my life back. Love you both.

Stephanie, thank you for giving all you had.

Mr. R. for believing in me and playing all four quarters,
thank you, sir.

My old friend Kate who gave me the precious gift of my dog Jack.
Jack was looking for someone to save, he picked me...

Tony K., thanks for your trust and another great adventure.

Introduction

In this year of living dangerously, there were many people caught up in these life-changing events.

Amongst those included were family, friends, my community, and people across the country and abroad, many of whom I have never met.

In the following story, I tried to tell what I alone experienced. For many of these people, their own experiences were completely unique to them.

For some, their own lives were put on hold for the benefit of mine. To those special family and friends, a million thank-you's is not close to being enough.

All of them are my heroes!

Out of the night that covers me,
Black as the pit from pole to pole,
I thank whatever gods may be
For my unconquerable soul....

It matters not how strait the gate,
How charged with punishments the scroll,
I am the master of my fate:
I am the captain of my soul.

From Invictus, by William Ernest Henley
(*The Oxford Book of English*, Verse 1250-1918)

Prologue

Deep Captivity

Buca (pronounced boo-zah) prison in Izmir, Turkey, was a maximum-security lockdown with about fifteen hundred of the hardest, most badass prisoners on the planet. I was told later it was number three on Amnesty International's human rights "hit list." For years, Amnesty International had suspected this prison was the site of severe and unspeakable human rights violations. However, Amnesty's relentless efforts to gain some kind of access to this four-hundred-year-old dungeon was systematically denied. In the coming days and months, I would experience that abuse first hand.

My transfer day seemed to go on forever. I was shackled and stuffed into the back of a small, windowless military van with a thick, heavy, rancid smell that instantly made me gag. The endless, violent ride had me exhausted and numb by the time we arrived at the prison complex.

After the dreaded processing and the often-violent strip search, my descent started. I was taken through endless cell doors. Each gate slammed shut behind me with a heavy, solid clanging sound that produced a deep hollow ache going right down to my core. For whatever reason, I caught myself counting the nine heavy steel lockdowns, each one taking me farther down into the depths of this ominous place. My decent became evident by the heavy, putrid air and the single hanging light bulbs reflecting off the wet, dirty walls, giving the place a ghostly glow.

My forced march through this dark and filthy maze of tunnels led us to a huge locked steel gate. The guards were shouting at me in Turkish, as if I understood. Their anger and impatience were obvious. It took both men to open the enormous gate, and after hesitating, their huge hands shoved me inside. I found myself looking down a long, dark, wet tunnel. It appeared to be about the length of a football field. Reflex made me coil back as a violent shiver raced through my entire body, my knees instantly buckled as a crippling terror swept over me. I screamed inside my head "Where in Hell am I?!"

Every nerve ending was telling me this was without a doubt a very BAD, BAD PLACE! I struggled to get a grip on the reality of where I was. Trying to see down to the end of the darkness, I knew I was entering the worst place I would ever experience in my life.

The two guards brutally yanked me to my feet and started pushing me from behind, once again shouting in Turkish while prodding me with their thick batons, forcing me to jog between the grimy, dripping, concrete walls. Taking me deeper and farther down into this surreal Hellhole. I remembered thinking a Hollywood movie could not have made a more graphic set. The long dark corridor was thick with moisture and stench, with just a few spots of hanging lights.

As they trotted me past the cell block doors branching off like fingers from the tunnel, I could feel and hear the invisible faces wrestling to peer out. Their incessant, screaming in their foreign language severely rattled my nerves. The guard's commands became louder; the shouting and banging on steel gates was deafening. Roughly pushing me a few steps ahead, I realized they were putting this American captain on display.

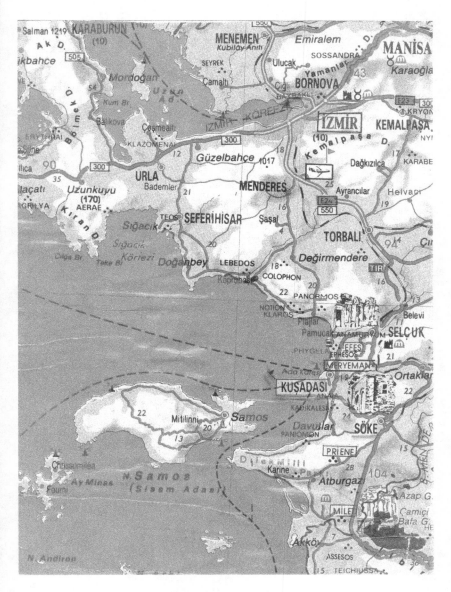

Turkish coastline, the towns in my story are on the map.

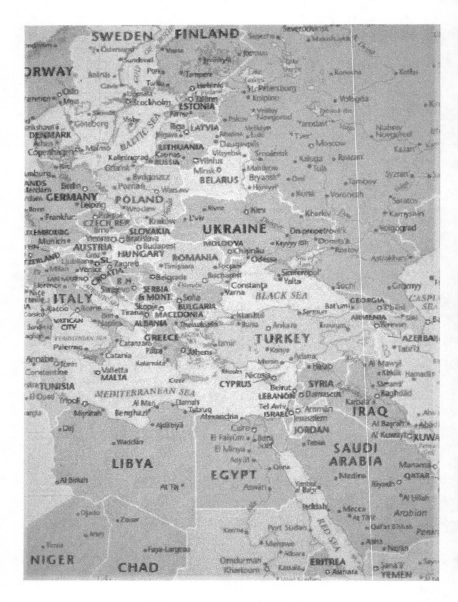

1

For the true sailor, it is often more dangerous in port than at sea.

I gazed out the small window on a hot, crystal clear day, and caught myself daydreaming. Looking back across oceans and decades, I saw a beach kid growing up with a lot of brothers and sisters in a modest military family in Southern California. Not a dime to spare but taught right from wrong. Hard work was a part of our family fabric, which led me here—at the age of forty-four— captain of one of the world's great mega yachts. I was responsible for navigating ships and crew across distant seas to foreign lands, halfway around the globe. The journey had been long, but the years passed quickly.

Knowledge and experience gained through the years had earned me the title of master on board the magnificent *Picante*. Hard work by everyone involved established her as one of the busiest and best motor yachts in the world. I considered it one of the elite jobs in our industry, and not just because I loved the ship herself, the world travel, great money, or professional crew. Good ownership was the most important factor for me as captain.

Mr. R. owned the *Picante*. We shared a passion for yachts and the adventures they provided. He gave me his respect and trust, allowing me to experience opportunities and challenges that very few captains ever know. He encouraged performance and always recognized achievement. I respected and liked him, enjoyed his praise, and very much wanted to please him. I was fortunate to have a life and career that was exactly what I wanted.

Traveling the Aegean Sea, I found myself in the port of Kusadasi (pronounced *koo-sha-dah-see*) on the west coast of Turkey in the summer of 1997. We were cruising the Greek islands with guests; we had dropped a group off on the island of Mykonos and sailed overnight to this Turkish port. We were scheduled to pick up another group of guests in four days.

After docking the *Picante* and making sure all was secure, I delivered the ship's papers to the Turkish customs official waiting on the dock. Later that morning, my first officer came up to the pilothouse and told me a police officer was on the dock, asking to speak to the captain. I had gotten no sleep because of the overnight trip in rough seas, so I was tired and annoyed with the intrusion. My ship's protocol when arriving in a new port was for crew to dress in formal uniforms. In Turkish society, uniforms gave the men who wore them a degree of authority. To them, the title of captain demanded respect. As an American captain of a large luxury yacht, I knew I would be a little intimidating to the Turkish officer who had been sent to speak to me.

So, in my crisp whites bearing the four stripes of captain, I marched down the ship's alleyway toward the stern. The noticeably young policeman had come up the gangway and was standing on the aft deck with my chief officer. I approached the uncomfortable group with obvious impatience. The Turkish officer's act of false authority was transparent as he struggled to meet my glare. I understood that I was to come with him to the port office. I made it clear I needed a few minutes to gather some things and headed back toward the pilothouse. He attempted to follow, but I abruptly turned and instructed him to wait for me on the dock.

Embarrassed, he meekly made his way back down the gangway. I thought his request unusual, but nothing that could not be taken care of quickly. After many years of sailing in and out of these remote ports, I had a reputation for rarely leaving my ship and going ashore. I knew I appeared somewhat unapproachable by the foreign vendors and local authorities, which made this request even more curious.

After two hours sitting in the small police office, nothing had been said to me about why I had been detained. I had sailed these waters for many years and was well known. For the port police to take me off my ship was strange. I was getting worried and started thinking of my options.

I felt the bulging wad of crisp one hundred-dollar bills in my pocket. An automatic reaction had made me take the money out of the ship's safe when the port authorities summoned me. Experience told me that, in this part of the world, it was wise to have some American dollars available. Sometimes, for no real reason, a payoff might be necessary, allowing us to go about our business. But if it were not appropriate in this situation, it could backfire, putting the *Picante* in trouble and possibly allowing it to be seized. To me, that was unthinkable.

My ship's agent had a serious and somber look on his face when he came into the office with the Turkish police captain. In his English translation, he told me they were taking me to the local jail, and that I would go before a tribunal judge tomorrow. I exploded, "What the hell for?!" I could feel my stomach doing one of those butterfly flips. He whispered that they did not give him any reason, only that my name came up on the computer during passport checks and they would not say what for.

With stomach churning and mind racing, I knew this was trouble. I needed to get the money back on board and figure out some sort of plan. Though I was sure they would not keep me very long, I had a lot of responsibilities and much to worry about. Little did I know.

The highest pendulum swing of a person's mental and physical limits is rarely reached in most people's lifetimes. In the year that followed, my emotional boundaries on that pendulum were stretched to just such extremes, taking me places I never could have imagined or even understood.

3

2

Turkey, Summer 1997

In retrospect, I realize I have been lucky with the hand I was dealt. High school football star, college scholarship, beach kid growing up in Southern California...

I started my career as a sailor in the late 1970s as a deckhand on the king of Malaysia's yacht. After a few weeks at sea, I knew this was what I wanted for my life and career. Having some luck and a bit of motivation enabled me to climb the ladder rapidly to the captain position. I loved what I was doing; the lifestyle and rewards were great. I had wonderful relationships with my family, friends, and the great people I spent time with along the way. They were people who loved me, and whom I had loved.

These were just some of the thoughts that came at me as I sat in a small cell in the seaport town of Kusadasi on the west coast of Turkey. I had brought the *Picante* to this port a few times and knew the port police. I was trying to figure out why I had been arrested and taken off the *Picante*, one of the most well-known and prestigious private yachts in the world. Life had been almost too good for me up to this point. Perhaps this was a way of balancing things out.

Certain thoughts played heavy on my mind. If I had chosen to act that night, the following year might have been very different for me. I was escorted to the small jail of Kusadasi that afternoon. Initially, I was not put into a cell, but allowed to sit in the front area where I could talk to Stephanie, our chef on board and my partner in life. The port police and local officials treated me with a great deal of respect. Being the captain of a large mega yacht was a prestigious position, and I could tell they felt uneasy about detaining me.

I managed to talk by cell phone with my boss, Mr. R. I could hear the intense worry in his voice, for his captain and boat half-way around the world. I explained that nobody could tell us—or would not tell us—why I was being detained. It certainly was not drugs or a problem with the vessel. I had not even seen a marijuana cigarette in twenty years, and the ship's papers were all in order. I felt bad not being able to give him any answers. I suggested a fill-in captain I knew who was available, although I did not think I would be detained much longer. He ended our brief conversation by telling me he would contact the American Consulate and try to get them involved. I knew if anyone could get to the bottom of this, it would be Mr. R.

I told Stephanie that she and the crew were to carry on with the duties that had to be done for the next guests. *Picante* was an elite charter vessel. People traveled halfway around the world and paid huge money to experience these ancient waters in utmost luxury and safety. They were always in search of an exotic, perfect vacation, and as their captain and host, it was my responsibility to make sure that happened, no matter what!

Later that night, I was shown into a small, unlocked cell where I could sleep. Lying there, my mind roamed. I caught myself thinking of people and events that were so far forgotten and irrelevant it surprised me. It was late, the night was hot, and still nobody was around. I thought I might be able to run right then! I could easily have gotten away. Looking back, *I wish I had!* However, there were many reasons I did not, the foremost being I had done nothing wrong!

The next day was filled with all kinds of calamity. Different people coming and going. None of them spoke English, and all of them wanted to be involved. The scene became more chaotic by the minute. I asked for a lawyer and was told several times it was not necessary. I took this as a good sign. We heard that the American Consulate people were coming down from Izmir. I was confident they would be able to resolve the problem, allowing me to resume my captain duties on board the *Picante*.

When they arrived, I was introduced to a pretty young Turkish woman, Jale Kaptaner, and a man named Randall Biggers, who I can honestly say without malice, and at least at that moment, was one of the ugliest men I had ever met. I was immediately disappointed. His attitude and appearance made it difficult to look at him when he talked. He was about forty, dark, rail thin, very gaunt, and had about five big moles on his face. Each mole had hair protruding straight out at least an inch. His decaying buckteeth did not add anything good to his looks. He also had perpetual spit at the corners of his mouth, and you could easily see he made no effort at grooming.

He told me I would be brought before a judge later. Nothing he could do, he said; he had to catch the bus back to Izmir. His condescending manner, combined with an arrogance that implied I must be guilty of something, really pissed me off. I reacted by grabbing him by the collar and forcing him against the wall. I told him in a low venomous voice, "You're not going anywhere. I want a lawyer!"

Nervous and stammering, he responded, "You don't need one, you're going to prison for forty days. It's the law." Straightening his shirt and making his way toward the door, he explained in a disinterested, cold tone that my name had been red flagged on the Interpol computer list, and they would not tell him why.

Stunned and confused, my feelings were magnifed by exhaustion and my body tight with the frustration of trying to understand what was going on in the grungy courtroom, to which I had finally been taken. I stood in the middle of a large, high-ceilinged room where every sound echoed. I could hear the lone typist banging away on his ancient typewriter, the sound vibrating right through me. I stared up at the judge; he wore a black robe with a bizarre stiff collar of bright red surrounding the back of his head and rising a good foot above him. I remember thinking that if he did not look so sinister, the scene might have been comical. The judge fit perfectly with his surroundings: the old wooden furniture and the smelly, gothic feeling of the courtroom itself.

I was deeply concerned about my vessel and the people on it, and I could not understand anything the judge and the people around him were saying. I had no interpreter, no nothing, except the sight of this person sitting at a long desk high above me. And then there was Stephanie, desperately trying to peer in through the door. She was not allowed in the courtroom because she was western, female, and did not have on the Muslim veil and clothes worn by most Turkish women. Two guards with automatic weapons stood firmly at the entrance, and no one was allowed in.

The next thing I knew, the judge was stamping papers and pounding the desk with a huge gavel. The echo of his gavel lent a penetrating feeling of finality to his words. (Little did I know how threatening the stamping of papers was to become for me.) He kept repeating the words, "Soke Prison, Soke Prison." (pronounced *Sir-kay*)

I had sailed this part of the world many times. I sensed what was coming, and my mind quickly snapped into gear. The guards in charge now were vastly different from the concerned port police from yesterday. I was rapidly escorted out and shackled in front of Stephanie. Her green eyes filled with tears of panic as I tried to reassure her this was all a big mistake and that I would be back on board very soon.

As I was shuffled away by the heavily armed guards, I tried to make her understand that I needed her more than ever. I shouted to her above the confusion, "Just keep the vessel and crew together!" I quickly gave her a series of commands, ranging from what to do with the ship's money to notifying the owner. I had to discharge my immediate responsibilities as captain and shake off my empathy for the terrifying emotions Stephanie must have been feeling as she watched me being shoved into the back of a foreign minivan with a couple of other Turkish prisoners. Desperately trying to see out the small window in the back of the van as it pulled away, I caught the frightened, lost look in her crying eyes. It hit me hard, extremely hard, releasing a moan that came from way down deep inside me.

The ride inland to the Turkish military prison seemed to take forever. I forced myself to focus on exactly what was happening. I was trying to absorb the big picture and think how to make the right decisions that would make things work down the road. With events taking control of my life, my thought process changed. I could not stop the intense worry about my vessel and particularly my boss, knowing the impact all this was going to have on so many people.

Soke prison was well inland from the coast. After the long torturous drive through the Turkish countryside, we arrived at the prison well after dark, and I did not see much of the surroundings when they unloaded us. The three of us prisoners were greeted sternly by a different group of military guards in different colored uniforms. But guards were guards, and they all had one thing in common: the ever-present automatic weapons.

We were roughly escorted through the huge metal gate, which slammed shut with a heavy clanging sound that sent a shudder right down my spine. Little did I know how dramatically my life would change in the next hour.

Once again, I noticed the dinginess and stale smell that comes from age and lack of maintenance. We were taken down a corridor and into a waiting area in front of an office door. The three of us sat on the cement floor, waiting to be processed. The two Turkish men were taken inside, and I could hear them loudly grunting and shouting in Turkish. When they were shoved out, I wanted to catch the eye of one of the men, but their heads were bowed in a humbled, subservient manner. They were led away, and I never saw either man again.

I sat on the cement floor with my head down. Two young military guards stood across from me, saying nothing. After several minutes, I was taken into an office where three uniformed men stood to one side and the commandant sat at the desk. My concern and responsibility I had felt toward the events taking place was suddenly replaced by a mind-numbing *terror* that gripped my insides.

The hot Turkish night descended on me like a thick wool blanket. My stomach ached; bile rose in my throat as I struggled to stay focused and alert. The annoying hum of a small fan in the corner had no effect on the heat, making everyone appear to be wearing a moist sheen. The filthy sweat of the guards left soaking, dirty stains that covered their entire uniforms.

An old wooden desk was littered with cigarette butts and empty Turkish coffee cups. A single light bulb hung from a cord, illuminating the brown smoke hanging from the ceiling. This ugly dull glow only added to the ominous feeling of the room, which turned out to be prophetic. The dirty office had a strange rancid odor, and much later I realized it did not come from the cigarettes or the coffee. It permeated from the guards themselves. The three of them were big and looked like brothers, with greasy black hair, droopy mustaches, and filthy, stained uniforms.

The commandant was smiling and speaking Turkish to me. The only word I understood was his heavily accented pronunciation of the word "American." He repeated this with a big wolfish smile, showing a row of yellow, stained teeth punctuated by a gigantic silver tooth that reflected light from the bulb above his head.

My panic was heightened by how truly dangerous my immediate situation felt. I understood that he wanted me to empty my pockets on the desk. I did this, and as he fingered through my belongings, one of the guards motioned for me to take off my shirt.

I started to unbutton it, but I guess they did not like the speed at which I was doing this.

From that moment on, nothing in my life would ever be the same. All three guards decided to undress me themselves. My shoes and pants were ripped off. I was whipped around and slammed against the brick wall, giving my head a good crack that started bleeding. Two of the guards roughly grabbed my arms and kicked my legs wide apart. With my face against the wall, the only thing I could see out of the side of my eyes was the third guard putting on rubber gloves.

That nauseous acid in my stomach rapidly climbed up my throat as panic and fear consumed my entire body. They were incredibly strong; I was helpless; my whole body was caught in a giant vice. I know I was screaming and struggling to get away, but I do not remember hearing myself.

When they were done with their brutal examination, I was spun around, unable to stand on my own and the painful grip of rough hands holding me up. My head was spinning, and I could taste the vomit in my throat as it trickled out the corners of my mouth. Searing pain slowly took over my senses, and a flood of pure hatred, unlike anything I had ever felt before, consumed me. My glare pierced the commandant sitting behind his desk, but he continued to grin as he motioned for me to get dressed.

Turkish prison authorities are infamous for their strip searches. Their expertise comes from centuries of practice, perfecting the barbaric ritual of dehumanizing and instilling complete humility on their victims. I realized later they had been particularly vicious with me, making an extra effort to welcome the American Captain.

3

It was the middle of the night by the time I was led through a small courtyard, pushed through a big metal door, and locked in a small cell with sixteen Turkish inmates. My mind and body were numb, but not enough to insulate me from the screaming and yelling of the Turkish prisoners caged inside this small prison cell. With the noise level deafening and all eyes staring at me, the shock to my mental focus was staggering.

The dramatic change in my circumstances hit me hard. I was leaving a world of wide-open freedom and entering a place where basic instincts prevailed. The bunks were stacked four high to the ceiling, and all of them were occupied. The cell was stifling hot and full of smoke. I huddled on the floor, my back to the steel door. The smell and confusion were unbearable. All I wanted to do was close my eyes and sleep, hoping that tomorrow everything would sort itself out.

The beating I had just received left me with a swollen face and bruised ribs, and the intense pain kept me awake. I reached inside the back of my jeans and realized I was bleeding from the brutal search. At that moment, it hit me that this ordeal was going to be about pure survival, and every other emotion faded as anger consumed me. Through that first night, many thoughts came and went, but something made me think of what a great old coach of mine once said to me after my final game: "Michael, you may not be the most talented player that ever played for me, but you are certainly one of the fiercest competitors." I knew that before this was all over, I would have to reach deep and find enough fight in me to survive.

The next morning, I had to force myself to snap out of an all-consuming depression. My anxiety over my ship, just twenty-four hours ago, had been replaced by the panic brought on by the dramatic change in my life and the radical difference in my environment.

My tension was broken slightly when one of the Turkish prisoners came to me, trying hard to communicate with no English at all. His name was Yilmaz, and he was a tall, dark, comical-looking fellow, which is exactly what he turned out to be. He insisted I take one of the top bunks next to the barred window. This prompted a ferocious shouting match with the Turk who occupied that space. Yilmaz climbed to the top and delivered a few mean, hard slaps, literally dragging the man off while every prisoner was shouting at the top of their lungs. His kindness to me was immeasurable, but I knew this was going to come back at me. I had made an enemy my first day in here.

I could only sit and watch this chaos play out and wonder how I had gotten there. It truly was a king-of-the-hill atmosphere, and I was getting an early glimpse at the lay of the land.

The next few days were a blur. I expected at any moment to be released. No one spoke English, and I obviously did not speak Turkish. I was forced to fall into the prison routine that began with a numbered roll call. In fact, that was my first Turkish word: the number three in line, or "ewch."

The stench of the open toilet, along with the ants, cockroaches, and spiders, was overwhelming—but the two worst things were the rats and the unrelenting noise. When it rained, the sewer right outside our cell would overflow. The smelly, brackish water would flood in through the cell door and other cracks in the ancient building, bringing with it a dozen or so Turkish rats. A few men would make a chaotic game out of chasing down and killing them. The others shouted and cheered at the spectacle, while placing bets. I could never get used to this, or to the constant cacophony of everyone shouting twenty-four hours a day within that cell. Looking down from my fourth-level bunk, I wondered if I had been put into a Turkish mental ward.

The loud broadcasting of Muslim prayers over loudspeakers from the mosques around the town prompted all the inmates to grab their little rugs and drop to their knees like robots. They did this prayer routine five times a day, and it became very irritating. The chanting from those mosque speakers gave me a creepy feeling that never went away.

Overall, conditions were diabolical. Sixteen, now seventeen men were stacked four-high inside a cell about 20' by 20'. In one back corner, behind a little brick wall about four feet high, was a hole in the floor with a short hose hanging from a hook. This was the toilet. No such thing as toilet paper; they did not use it. That is what the hose was for. Viewing each man's head from my fourth-floor bunk as they squatted over the open hole in the corner made me resist climbing down and crossing the room to use it. For the first three days, I just could not do it. Eventually I had to, however, and it became matter of fact. It was necessary to fall to the level of this existence to survive.

I tried to stay to myself, although that was next to impossible because I was *the American*, which was very unusual. I doubt any of the other men had ever met an American. Yilmaz did his best to be my friend, guiding me through the prison routine and keeping other inmates away from me. He was a man of deceptive appearance. He came across as comical, forever talking, and I could see the others found him very funny. However, if there was any serious disturbance—which seemed to occur daily with seventeen men in this tiny cell—he would transform into the iron fist. He had no problem delivering a ferocious barrage on anyone he felt deserved it.

Yilmaz became my good friend and went out of his way to help me if he could. It did not seem to matter that we could not speak each other's language; we managed to communicate. As the months passed, I learned that he had been in the Turkish military.

He had stolen a gasoline truck and was selling fuel to the local villagers at a price that amounted to giving it away. After I came to know him, the nature of his crime did not surprise me.

I understood he wanted to know all about the United States. He loved everything American, and I realized I was the first American he had met in person. He dreamed of going there one day. He was just the kind of man who would do well in America, if he ever made it. He had been in this place five years and still had many more years before his release, if ever. He was twenty-five years old.

In a Turkish prison like Soke, the guards did not interfere with inmates. Any problems inmates had were taken care of between themselves. I knew from the first day I would have to deal with the Turk whose bunk I had taken over. He had to save face somehow. Tension increased, as he and his few friends had made it clear that something had to be done to me. Yilmaz was on my side, but the fact that I could not understand what anyone said added tremendously to my fear. I was frightened of a confrontation but knew I had to mentally prepare for something to happen. The restless tension inside me was starting to bulge and ready to burst.

Something had to give, and finally it did. I realized the only chance I had was to react hard and fast the moment he made his move. It happened just as I was leaving the hole in the ground, they called the toilet. I wanted to just get back to the sanctuary of my top bunk, but he stood directly in front of me in the middle of the cell. He was a little taller than me, of average build, and about forty years old. A dark swarthy face with dark eyes made him look very menacing. It became quiet as everyone knew what was going to happen. All except me.

Every hair stood up on my body; the adrenaline pumped; and that deep scared feeling made me shake. He was shouting and waving his arms about with his back turned to me, playing to his cheering audience. Just as he turned, ready to spit in my face, a reflex made me tense, and not realizing what I was doing, I struck. My right fist cracked on his jaw and he went down. To my surprise, as well everyone else's, he was unconscious. I had knocked him out!

There was dead silence, and I felt like everything was moving in slow motion. Then in an instant, the cell erupted. In the confusion, I scrambled up to my top bunk, struggling to come out of whatever zone I was in. My right thumb hurt, and I was trying hard to stop my shaking. Looking down at the chaos, I spotted Yilmaz looking up at me with a huge grin on his face, giving me a small nod. Somehow, what I had done was right in this alien world, but I was petrified at the thought of the Turk or someone else climbing the four bunks during the night and attacking me while I slept.

During the following days, it appeared I had passed some sort of test or initiation. I learned later that I was expected to take the insult and let the Turk save face. However, someone forgot to tell me. Besides, I do not know any American that would take a spit in the face without reacting with their fists. The Turkish do not fight or slug it out. They slap each other or figure out a way to exchange insults in order to save face. They were stunned by how I had reacted, thinking all of America must be this way. As far as I was concerned, they were damned right, and I was proud of it.

Other inmates tried to make conversation or offer me tea. I guess I had gained some respect, but all I wanted was to be out. At least the tension had passed, and I no longer was bothered by that Turk or any of the other inmates.

I was now living on the fourth bunk on top, three feet from the ceiling, next to the only barred window in the cell. I soon realized how fortunate I was that Yilmaz had given me this bunk. Observing the men from my small sanctuary, I saw that everyone chained-smoked hand-rolled Turkish cigarettes. The smoke filled the top four feet of the cell, and just hung there like a dirty cloud. The hot, humid air was heavy and still, but being next to the only window in the room, I managed to get enough fresh air for relief.

I had no reading material, no English conversation. The hours were lonely and anxious. The waves of panic and isolation made me begin to search for something to work on. A spider that had set up camp just outside my barred window occupied my imagination for hours and hours. I watched him build his own personal fortress, methodically and with discipline. Throughout his daily routine, he showed characteristics of strength, independence, and a huge desire to live. He was focused, dedicated, and worked relentlessly with purpose every single day. When catching his prey, he would make his way out to the edges of his web and quickly wrap it inside his silk, then drag it back, and hang it upside down, saving it for later. I could not help but notice his patience and skill. He took no breaks, being driven by his passion to overcome whatever odds were against him.

I realized he also was in a prison and would do whatever it took to survive. He was his own provider and understood this completely. I wondered if he had that deep, lonely feeling of it being him against the world. I imagined his and my own existence were the same. Perhaps he was teaching me what I had to do for myself.

My ship had to leave for two weeks with a new captain and guests. Stephanie had to sail with them. The two weeks passed, and every day felt like a year. I was completely cut off from everyone. There was no way to communicate, and I was not even sure if my family and friends knew where I was. I still did not know why I had been arrested. The panic and anxiety ravaging my stomach was just starting to take its toll. It was only a fraction of what was to come.

After the two-week voyage, Stephanie left the boat and returned to Turkey. With help from our ship's agents, along with bribe money passed to the prosecutor, they eventually let her in for a visit. She was told not to wear her normal American clothes to the prison, and they insisted she wear a scarf and the long dress of Muslim women. When I finally saw her, I had to peer through a small barred metal door to see her face. We were only allowed a few minutes, and I could see she was completely distraught.

In the Turkish prison system, you are not issued uniforms, there is no cafeteria food, and what you are able to hold onto is all you have. So, I must have looked ragged to her, wearing the same dirty clothes I had been arrested in, my eyes sunken and dazed. But for me, seeing her was unbelievable. I was flooded with relief, thinking she would tell me that I would be released at any moment. However, I knew instantly when I looked into her eyes that this would not happen. She was so sad, and those eyes once again filled with crystal tears. She too was living a nightmare. Those few minutes passed quickly, but she managed to explain the few facts she knew.

Mr. R. had learned that the Interpol warrant originated in Greece in 1991, six years earlier. As soon as she said this, I was stunned, but I knew immediately what had happened.

She brought many things for me: food, jeans, jacket, and some writing materials, asking me to write down what I recalled about that time in Greece. Mr. R. and the people trying to help me needed to know what I could remember of the events from those years. She said she would not leave without me. Stephanie never knew this, but at that moment I loved her more than ever. I was comforted by the fact that she was close by, but the anxiety and stress were increasing.

4

I was unable to sit up in my fourth-floor nest because of how close I was to the smoke-stained ceiling. So, I laid down and closed my eyes, going back to 1991, remembering the people and events and trying to make sense of why I had been arrested. It was necessary to explain to my friends and supporters how I came to be in Greece in the first place. I started writing down what had happened ten years before, beginning in 1981.

After living and working on the king of Malaysia's yacht for almost two years, I left the Far East for the south of France. I was lucky to land one of the most sought-after jobs on board a well-known and beautiful 188' motor yacht. This vessel was owned by a wealthy Arab family and spent summers cruising the western Mediterranean. It would go south to Greece for the winter months.

In the early 1980s, I met some wonderful people in Greece and soon established a land base to come home to in winter. Through most of the 1980s, work took me all over the world, but I always kept my residence in Greece. In 1990, I decided to take a job as captain on board a 90' sailing yacht, which was based in Greece. This was different for me, but I wanted to spend some time near my home and work in these waters.

A couple of my friends who worked the waterfront in Greece tried to warn me about the Greek owner of the yacht, but after going through the interview process, he seemed okay to me. The boat was beautiful, but it had been neglected and needed some time in the shipyard to bring her back. This was my area of expertise, and over the following months I worked to refit and restore the vessel's systems.

By spring, the boat was ready, and the itinerary seemed perfect. The owner would only come onboard for the month of August and we would sail the Greek islands. As the weeks passed, however, I realized he was on board a lot more than just in August. It was certainly his prerogative as owner, but I started to see a dark and nasty side to this man.

He had gained some wealth, and with his bullish manner, made sure everyone knew it. He was a fifty-something guy with a paunch. He had dark hair, dark eyes, and a very loud voice. I could tell he fancied himself something of an international playboy. His twenty-one-year-old girlfriend was always in tow and was often the target of his rudeness. The small group of guests that traveled with him were always the same people. I actually got to know and even like them, but I felt a little sad watching each one take his abuse at different times. I guess they had their own reasons for putting up with it. I tried to ignore most of this and always kept a professional distance.

As the year passed, I worked hard to maintain and improve the boat. He recognized that I was a capable and knowledgeable captain and knew I had experience sailing the Caribbean. He wanted to know everything about sending his boat across the Atlantic to spend the winter months cruising those islands.

By August of '91, he and his group had already been onboard for several weeks. The Greek's rudeness had become more frequent. He even yelled at other boaters for the smallest of errors. I sensed his resentment because of the familiarity and friendliness his group extended toward me.

Our season was ending in the Greek islands, and the owner had not talked anymore about sending the boat across to the Caribbean. I assumed he had changed his mind, which was fine with me, as I planned to leave the boat after laying her up for the winter.

The day he and his guests left the boat, he pulled me aside and told me to get the vessel ready for the trip to the Caribbean. I told him we would need to leave in October. Many things had to be done, and during the next several weeks we worked hard to finish the work. I assembled a delivery crew and set our departure date.

About a week before our scheduled departure, I had a final meeting with the Greek owner. He informed me that he was going out of the country on business. He wanted to go over our routing plans again. I planned to sail straight through to the Cape Verde islands off the African coast and catch the trade winds across the Atlantic Ocean to the Caribbean island of Barbados. We ended our meeting, and he wished me good sailing and gave me ship's provisioning money. We knew it would be difficult to communicate, but I said I would try to call him when we reached the Verdes in Africa.

Everything was in order. The ship's debarkation papers were stamped by custom's officials, giving us authority to leave Greek waters. I estimated that it would take about five weeks to reach the Caribbean, providing we had good wind and sailed straight through.

We were six days out of Greece, off the North African coastline of Tunisia, not far from the Straits of Gibraltar and out of the Mediterranean Sea, when we hit a patch of the doldrums, which means no wind at all.

I decided to start the engine and motor through the lull, hoping we would find wind farther west. We were unable to start the engine and determined that the starter motor was bad. The next day, the wind picked up enough for us to change course and make a heading for the city of Tunis on the North African coast, where we had hoped to make the necessary repairs. I knew the country of Tunisia was not a normal stopping point for foreign flag yachts. It had a strict Muslim society and being an American during the Gulf War had me a little apprehensive.

I was able to reach Tunisian customs by radio. After a long and strained conversation, with my terrible broken French, I managed to convey our difficulties and ask for dockage. A small police skiff met us outside the port entrance of Tunis. We dropped our sails and secured their line to our bow, and they towed us through a maze of rusted old ships and ancient Arab working boats called dhows.

The busy and confused movements of all these boats along with the stiff and official manner of the customs authorities made us all feel strange and nervous. After tying the boat off, I followed normal procedures and handed over ship's transit papers and passports to the port authorities. A short while later, a group of policemen returned and instructed all of us to come with them. We were being arrested. They took us to a local jail and locked us up in a small, dark cell. We were held overnight, all of us deeply worried about what was going to happen next.

In the morning, we were transported to the office building of the Interpol police. I was interviewed by their officers and learned why we were being detained. They informed me that the yacht had been reported stolen. Disbelieving, I told him that could not be possible. I protested strongly to the authorities that our papers were in order and pleaded for them to contact the Greek owner. I was left alone in one of the offices, trying to understand what was happening.

When an officer returned, he told me the theft warrant had originated with my Greek owner. Their news stunned me; at first, I did not believe it. But after listening to their explanations, I realized it was true. My fear soon turned to anger at the nasty Greek owner. I could not understand why he was doing this.

We spent the next several hours being interrogated by Interpol investigators. Finally, at the end of the day, the chief Interpol Officer sat down and informed me of the facts. He had no explanation for the Greek owner's motive but told me that the crew and I were free to go. He said that the ship's transit papers were all in order, which gave me, as the captain, full authority to move the vessel. Legally, he could not detain us any longer, but he suggested we leave his country as soon as possible.

After being separated most of the day from the rest of my crew, I was now able to explain what had taken place. We were all disgusted and angry about what we had gone through. I suggested we get on the first available flight out. Without hesitation, I left the Greek's boat in Tunisia.

Over ten years of being in this business, this was my first experience of working for a bad owner. On the flight out, I had time to analyze what had happened. I had heard stories about bad owners from various crew on other yachts, and I decided to dismiss him and this whole experience.

Lying in my Turkish prison cell, I still could not understand why this had surfaced six years later. During those six years, I had captained large yachts all around the world, sailing in and out of many foreign ports without a single problem. I could only hope Mr. R. and my family would get to the bottom of this awful ordeal and just get me out.

5

We were allowed into the small courtyard a couple hours every day, and I forced myself to pace back and forth during this time. The stages of psychological change a person goes through when imprisoned are well documented, and I was experiencing the first—severe anxiety and panic, which would soon be replaced by anger.

I slowly became harder and more resilient. They made it exceedingly difficult for Stephanie to visit; each time it cost money. She was only allowed a few visits and brought news of everything people were doing worldwide to help me. This included my boss, Mr. R., whose life had been put on hold. Only later did I learn how much he had done, and the vast resources he had summoned to help me. Everyone involved was getting a crash course on our State Department policies, which basically have no mandate to assist Americans arrested abroad.

My family's contact at the consulate in Ankara, Turkey, was none other than Randall Biggers. I am not joking when I say he was truly one of the physically ugliest humans I have ever seen. He turned out to be just as ugly inside, creating roadblocks for my family and Mr. R. at every turn.

It is widely known that, no matter what nationality you are, everyone in trouble in a foreign land tries to contact the British Embassy. Here there was also the completely incomprehensible, disorganized Turkish bureaucratic system—a quagmire of people eagerly waiting to exploit the misfortunes of others, along with ruthless scumbags who surfaced with promises of release for cash.

These things and many more were some of the problems Stephanie, my family, and friends were trying to deal with.

They had found me a lawyer named Azra Immeler, and she was to visit soon. Looking back, that name conjures up a feeling of pure hatred. When she came to visit, I was escorted out to meet her. My first impression was that she was well-past middle age. She was dressed in a 1960s dress that was much too tight around her protruding stomach. It was low cut and revealed fat, fleshy breasts. She wore spiked heels and ruby red lipstick. I sat across from her thinking to myself, "You've got to be kidding me." But looks are not everything. I tried to keep an open mind.

Twenty minutes after she started talking to me in English, heavily mixed with Turkish, I knew I was in deep, deep trouble. Throughout the entire interview, she spoke incessantly about herself and how well connected she was. When she abruptly got up to leave, she told me in her awful accent and broken English, "Do not worry, Michael. Three days you will be out. Three days you will be out."

That is when I became truly worried about my situation.

Of course, I did not get out in three days. In fact, I did not even see her for two more weeks. Stephanie paid her a lot of my money, and she pretended she was helping but in fact she was doing nothing. Then came the official news that they could not hold me more than forty days. The emotional roller-coaster I was on as I waited for that fortieth day really took a toll on me. I lost a lot of weight, and the stress was unbearable. Azra gave Stephanie and my family every indication that I would be released on the fortieth day.

On the fortieth day, the expectations of me, my family, and Stephanie were very high. Thinking the end was finally here, Stephanie was at the prison waiting for me. The air in our cell was thick with excitement and anticipation. Yilmaz and a few others were happy for me and made a fuss, trying to make me look half-way decent, but late in the afternoon, news came that they were not going to release me. I was *devastated*! I could only imagine the emotional crash Stephanie was also experiencing. She could not bring herself to come inside and see me.

Azra came in to tell me what had happened. My filthy appearance and the fact that my blood was boiling startled her. She knew that I knew she had been lying to Stephanie and my family. I could see right through her.

After that day, because she was aware of my feelings, she stayed away and rarely came to see me. She asked them for more money, promising to get me out with another plan. I could not communicate to Stephanie and my family what she was doing. Looking back, I realize they were becoming very frustrated, but the thought of trying to find someone else to help was too much to handle.

Several thousand dollars had been given to Azra, which probably bought her an extremely comfortable life in Turkey. At one point, she came up with a plan for me to marry a Turkish woman, which would somehow aid in my release. I was unable to communicate how she was deceiving everyone. I had sunk to rock bottom, and the emotional fall crushed me. Nobody knew or could tell us what would happen next.

My family and friends had tried to stay low key in the hope it would not rattle the Turkish government. That plan changed after the Azra fiasco, and they solicited the help of Ross Perot, several congressmen, State Department officials, and many other authorities. But most importantly, a former guest on our vessel, someone I had become friendly with, came to our aid.

Dustin Hoffman knew powerful businesspeople in Turkey, and he put his reputation on the line for me. The Turkish media spun into a frenzy when news got out that Dustin Hoffman had spoken on my behalf. He truly is one of the nicest, most intelligent men I have ever met. Overnight, Steph and I became front page news on every Turkish newspaper.

Inside, I had no access to any news or information from the outside, but Yilmaz and a few other men got excited and were able to tell me that their families said I was on Turkish television and in their newspapers. That week when their relatives came to visit, I noticed they were all trying to peer into the courtyard to see me, gesturing and waving like I was a celebrity.

After a week of international attention, the Turkish prison bureaucracy became very agitated. The prison guards came in the middle of the night and jerked me out of the cell. I was unceremoniously paraded to the infamous commandant's office, where I stood in front of him once again, silent and afraid, the sweaty, filthy guards on both sides of me.

He was looking down at a Turkish newspaper with my picture on the front page. Without warning, he erupted into a furious tirade, screaming at me in Turkish and pounding on the desk. By that time, I had learned a couple of swear words in Turkish, and he used every one of them. I'm not sure what I was exactly thinking, but I made the big mistake of smiling at him. His head almost exploded as he frantically swung his arms and screamed what sounded like an order.

The two guards slammed me to the cement floor and pinned me down. The commandant came around his desk and viciously stared down at me, not saying a word. He angrily motioned to the guards, and they roughly yanked me to my feet and escorted me back to my cell. I am not sure if fear is what I felt, but I did know my life inside prison was going to get even tougher.

The people trying to help me started to understand that people in this part of the world did not think like we did. Common sense did not apply to their way of life or the way they understood the world. Everyone at home was getting desperate. They were getting the idea that I was going to be spending a long, long time in this prison. Nothing they did or anyone they talked to could do anything to help. They knew it was a matter of money but did not know the contacts or which avenue to take.

Out of nowhere, a man appeared who presented all the right credentials to make it happen. Certain plans were put in motion. I got word that a Turkish lawyer with political ties would be visiting me, and with his connections and forty-five thousand dollars, he could get me out. The clandestine scheme was hatched like something right out of a Tom Clancy novel.

However, once again when this man got in to see me, I knew something was wrong. Right away, his demeanor and appearance came across like a B-rated bad actor. He showed up wearing black cowboy boots, black jeans, and a black shirt unbuttoned down to his fat stomach. He was trying to give me the impression that he was some slick American cowboy. If he only knew how ridiculous and out of place he looked. But my hopes were raised when I saw how the commandant treated him with respect. Later, I learned that respect equals the amount of money paid.

His plan was that a doctor friend of his would get me transferred to the hospital. From there, an elaborate escape plan would come into play. It is interesting how even the most ridiculous and outrageous ideas made sense to me. I was so desperate to get out, I would have tried anything. But the end result was that we didn't hear from him for several weeks, until he made contact with Stephanie and demanded another forty-five thousand dollars, saying that if we didn't pay I would spend the rest of my life in a Turkish prison.

This shattering news was passed on to my boss. He, in turn, made a phone call, and this man was never heard from again. I suspect he was paid a visit by some goodfellas, but I never knew. Paying forty-five thousand dollars and not getting out really sent me spinning. My life's savings was being thrown away, and I had no control over anything. The psychological damage was possibly irreversible.

Anxiety and panic rose dramatically inside me. This kind of stress was something I had never experienced. I knew it set the cycle for all the stages one goes through in such a situation. It's well documented, and I knew I was following the pattern to a tee. The thing is, I would have paid anything...forty-five thousand, ninety thousand, anything...if the plan would work.

Stephanie had my power of attorney and sold off a rental property I owned just to keep things moving. Another plan was hatched. My family and boss were able to reach Ross Perot and explain my plight. He investigated and agreed to do as much as he could. He put Mr. R. in touch with a group of people who were willing to help, again for a price. A couple of weeks later, two mercenary-type guys showed up at Soke Prison and somehow were able to get in to see me.

This in itself was remarkable. They were a couple of good old boys from Texas, but these men were not rookies. Soke is a military prison in the middle of nowhere. The plan was to launch a commando raid to break me out. One of the men told me to sit tight, and when I heard the password *Geronimo* the plan would be on.

A few days later, he got in to see me again. He told me that because of the stronghold, people would probably be hurt. I contemplated this, and as ridiculous as it sounded, everyone was deadly serious, especially me. They decided it was too dangerous, forcing them to call it off. Once again, there went several thousand dollars.

The situation was getting very strange and difficult for Stephanie. Living in a foreign land, long taxi rides into the night to meet strange people who made promises that they could help for a price. Being spied on by the authorities and getting international attention had really started to take its toll on her.

The heat of summer was over, and the cold weather of fall and winter were setting in. I had not seen her in about two weeks. When I came to the prison gate and peered through at her, it took my breath away. She looked rail thin. Her face was gaunt, and the dark circles beneath her eyes made my heart ache. I fiercely exclaimed, "Stephanie, get home! Just go home!" The worry of something happening to her or even being arrested was something I could not handle. I kept repeating to her, "Just go home!"

She came back a few days later to say goodbye, promising she would never give up on me. I tried to sound strong, but my voice was cracking. I assured her I would survive, and she should go home. Once again, those beautiful green eyes flooded with tears, and we both cried. Just as the guards stepped up to escort her out of the prison, she quickly motioned for me to put my ear to the iron gate. She whispered, "Michael Churchward, you are the strongest man I have ever known. You will survive." I fought to choke back the sob.

Five minutes later, a note was passed into me. Just one sentence that read, "Please don't give up. I will never, never give up on you. Love Stephanie." Reading through blurry, wet eyes, a surge of strength shivered through my body and I swore that somehow, someway, I would get myself home.

I had been in Soke Prison about four months at this point, and the pressure was mounting on the Turkish officials. Our State Department and the international media were creating a headache for the Turkish prison bureaucracy. Their solution was to transfer me to another prison, Buca (pronounced Boozah) prison in Izmir. This news brought shock and dismay to the few friends I had made inside Soke. They were able to communicate to me that it was a very bad place. I thought to myself, *how much worse could it get?* Little did I know, it could get a lot worse.

A few weeks earlier, I had told Stephanie to get five hundred dollars, and through our ship's agents, have them get it to Yilmaz's family. They were extremely poor, and that kind of money was enormous for them. It was the least I could do for the help he had given me. When his family came to visit, he was talking with them through the large iron gate. He turned and motioned for me to come over. It seemed all his relatives saw me as some sort of celebrity, and I realized Yilmaz had told them I was leaving Soke Prison. They all crowded around the small opening on the other side of the locked door and wanted to say good-bye to me. His little old mother, with her wise and weathered face, was particularly sad. Being sweet with her regard and concern, she put her hand to the iron gate and wanted to touch my face. I realized Yilmaz had become a good friend and leaving him was going to be hard.

My transfer became a media circus in front of Soke Prison. The Turkish TV news was there, along with several other news media, all shouting as I was shackled and brought out to the waiting van. All I remember is the chaos and the cameras clicking. As we pulled away in the police van, people chased us in their small foreign cars and little mopeds, trying to take pictures.

Several hours later, we arrived at a sprawling huge complex. They escorted me in through the front door of the office buildings, where once again the media were waiting. They almost seemed proud to be a part of this entire calamity. I found myself again in an office, only this time standing in front of a well-dressed man in a suit who smiled and spoke a few words to me in Turkish. I would later have another meeting with this man (who turned out to be the director of the prison) that would not be so pleasant.

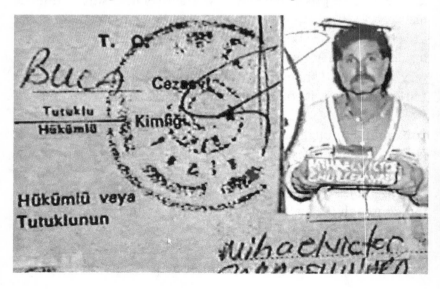

6

Buca (pronounced *boo-zah*) prison in Izmir, Turkey, was a maximum-security lockdown with about fifteen hundred of the hardest, most badass prisoners on the planet. I was told later it was number three on Amnesty International's human rights "hit list." For years, Amnesty International had suspected this prison was the site of severe and unspeakable human rights violations. However, Amnesty's relentless efforts to gain some kind of access to this four-hundred-year-old dungeon was systematically denied. In the coming days and months, I would experience that abuse firsthand.

My transfer day seemed to go on forever. I was shackled and stuffed into the back of a small, windowless military van with a thick, heavy, rancid smell that instantly made me gag. The endless, violent ride had me exhausted and numb by the time we arrived at the prison complex.

After the dreaded processing and the often-violent strip search, my descent started. I was taken through endless cell doors. Each gate slammed shut behind me with a heavy, solid clanging sound that produced a deep hollow ache going right down to my core. For whatever reason, I caught myself counting the nine heavy steel lockdowns, each one taking me farther down into the depths of this ominous place. My decent became evident by the heavy, putrid air and the single hanging light bulbs reflecting off the wet, dirty walls, giving the place a ghostly glow.

My forced march through this dark and filthy maze of tunnels led us to a huge locked steel gate. The guards were shouting at me in Turkish, as if I understood. Their anger and impatience were obvious. It took both men to open the enormous gate, and after hesitating, their huge hands shoved me inside. I found myself looking down a long, dark, wet tunnel. It appeared to be about the length of a football field. Reflex made me coil back as a violent shiver raced through my entire body, my knees instantly buckled as a crippling terror swept over me. I screamed inside my head "Where in Hell am I?!"

Every nerve ending was telling me this was without a doubt a very, BAD, BAD PLACE! I struggled to get a grip on the reality of where I was. Trying to see down to the end of the darkness, I knew I was entering the worst place I would ever experience in my life.

The two guards brutally yanked me to my feet and started pushing me from behind, once again shouting in Turkish while prodding me with their thick batons, forcing me to jog between the grimy, dripping, concrete walls. Taking me deeper and farther down into this surreal Hellhole. I remembered thinking a Hollywood movie could not have made a more graphic set. The long dark corridor was thick with moisture and stench, with just a few spots of hanging lights.

As they trotted me past the cell block doors branching off like fingers from the tunnel, I could feel and hear the invisible faces wrestling to peer out. Their incessant, screaming in their foreign language severely rattled my nerves. The guard's commands became louder; the shouting and banging on steel gates was deafening. Roughly pushing me a few steps ahead, I realized they were putting this American captain on display.

The guards stationed at each cellblock made the Soke guards seem clean and well dressed. A rancid, mildew smell mushroomed off them, along with something else. These men were sneering and mean in ways that I would only later really understand.

I was nervous and frightened. It was a different environment with different faces, and I struggled to understand what was going on around me. We came to the last cellblock. The keys rattled as they unlocked the heavy metal door. From what little Turkish I understood, I could tell the guards were having a good laugh between them about the American captain. They had never seen an American in here before, let alone someone who was in their newspapers. I did not get the feeling it was a friendly laugh.

The crowd of prisoners separated as I was shoved inside. I came face to face with a tall, handsome man standing out among the other riffraff. With a big smile, he said, "Welcome to our home!"

It stunned me. He spoke the most perfect Oxford English. He was dressed in a brilliant white polo shirt with the collar turned up, and white billowy pants, and even slippers. I glanced at the other men. They were all wearing torn and mismatched rags for clothes. Their dirty and unkempt appearance made them look like pirates. Perhaps they were this man's personal band of scallywags. Later, I learned that was not far from the truth.

He said they had a place for me. I followed as he guided me down the hallway, passing several cells. Stopping, and without taking his eyes off mine, he motioned to someone inside. A man got up without a word and brushed by us, leaving a vacant, rusty, steel cot for me. I did not know it then, but this man, Daoud, would have a huge impact on my stay in Buca.

The cellblock was a long, narrow corridor completely enclosed with absolutely no access to the outside. It had twelve cells on one side; each cell had nothing but three rusty cots and a hole in the floor for the toilet. Only the cellblock door was locked. There was no way out. The prisoners in this block consisted of Pakistanis, Russians, Iraqis, Iranians, and Kurds. Most were accused terrorists. The place felt like death; the inmates had nothing, maybe a thin blanket, and their clothing ragged and used up. These pathetic men all looked the same: gaunt, gray, and ill. Death, disease, and despair were in abundance in this lost place.

I learned later that some of these prisoners had not been brought before a court for seven years. They were completely cut off from their families, and nobody could do anything for them. It was a lost world of forgotten souls. I felt like I was just one prison gate away from hell itself, and I soon realized the danger was not the other inmates. It was this dreadful and sinister place where men were left to die. I was deeply frightened to find myself here but determined to find a way out.

The next few days I gravitated to Daoud. He had managed to isolate himself on his own personal island amid this incredible squalor. I was utterly amazed at how he had decorated his dwelling with hanging Turkish tapestries that cordoned off two bunks he had pushed together to create his own personal tent complete with pillows and niceties, which were kept spotless by the two boys who lived with him. His cell resembled some sort of harem.

I was invited inside to sit and have tea, also provided by one of his young friends. I was fascinated and comforted by his genuine hospitality, along with the profound luxury of being able to speak English.

In the following weeks, I spent many hours in Daoud's cell listening to stories about his life. He was Iranian, about forty, with silver hair ,tall with a dark complexion. He had an infectious laugh and a quick wit that offered humor and provided a little medicine for my soul. Educated in England, he spoke several languages. His career had consisted of many businesses, all of them illegal. From his early years in Los Angeles as an art thief to the present day as one of the bigger opium and hashish smugglers in Afhanistan, taking his contraband across the Iraqi mountains and into the ports of Turkey.

He explained that he was only taking a rest. He would probably be here another year maybe two, and then his people would pay for his release. I believed him. There were no TVs or newspapers, and no communication with the outside world. Yet he knew my story and told me of press reports about the American captain being held inside the terrible and infamous Buca Prison.

Men were thrown inside this place and forced to survive any way they could. There was nothing here, nothing at all, and if you had nothing, even existing was difficult to the extreme. The conditions were something you would not believe unless you experienced it firsthand, and as far as I ever learned, nobody was allowed inside Buca Prison unless they were going to stay for a while. Certainly, no human rights organization was allowed in. Daoud told me that I was the only American he had ever heard of to spend time in Buca.

There was virtually no food. Twice a day they brought a giant vat of yellow soup, and in the evening, they brought red soup. Daoud warned me not to eat it. He had food smuggled in and often invited me to join him.

The two young Iranian boys were no older than sixteen. They were his personal concubines and lived with him in his cell. These boys were completely lost to their families and had no future and very little hope. Because he took care of them, they catered to his every need and were completely loyal to him. I later realized they would protect and even die for him. Knowing of my growing friendship with Daoud, the young boys also started to look after me.

Fridays became special because we were allowed to shower. In Turkey, they call it the hamam. The giddiness it brought to these hard men made me smile. We all looked forward to this, as each cellblock, one by one, was taken downstairs to a giant enclosure where steaming hot water came out of small spigots positioned about waist high along the wall. This created a thick, steamy fog that was difficult to see through, an almost peaceful and surreal atmosphere. The guards were given cigarettes to look the other way or to disappear. This is where the men had sex. It was incredibly open and uninhibited. When you live in a place like that, inhibitions fall away. For some, it was a reason to stay alive if only for a brief time.

Daoud always insisted I take one of his boys to help me bathe. He promised me I would enjoy the experience. I initially resisted. I did not want to be a part of this place. I did not belong here. As I got to know and trust Daoud, I learned to look forward to the hamam and enjoy the short time during which I felt safe knowing someone was watching my back. It allowed me to drift and dream. This experience once a week provided nourishment for my soul, letting me hang onto my shrinking thread of hope.

I was completely cut off from everyone. There was no way to communicate with anyone on the outside. I had been in this place about two weeks when I first experienced the full brutality of this system. A Kurdish inmate who was considered a political prisoner and a well-known individual on our block was a constant target of the prison authorities' wrath. He was on a hunger strike (like there was anything to eat anyway!), protesting the fact that he had not been brought before any kind of court in four years!

The guards came without notice and with a speed and force that was truly frightening. They dragged him down the cellblock and out. He was carried back the next day and did not come out of his cell for quite a while. He could not walk, and his feet were black and blue and swollen to twice their size.

Daoud told me they stripped him naked, with his hands and ankles shackled together behind him. They hung him upside-down and beat the bottoms of his feet and ass. I was told the pain is excruciating. I worried, thinking at some point I might have to endure the same. After several weeks, things were getting very desperate. I knew if I stayed in this place I would eventually die. Lack of proper food was taking its toll on my body. I developed sores, and my hair was starting to fall out, not to mention that I was chronically sick. Daoud informed me the American Consulate had started making noises and was insisting on seeing me. I could only guess how he knew all of this.

I borrowed a scrap of paper from Daoud and wrote a letter to Stephanie in the hope I might be able to smuggle it out. The letter detailed some of the human rights abuses and conditions inside Buca. Shortly after that, I was brought up out of the long tunnels to a small room where the American consul in Izmir had gotten in to see me. Her name was Jale Kaptaner. The very first day of my arrest, she had come to see me with the other man, Randall Biggers. She was a young, attractive Turkish lady who seemed to really want to help me.

I was brought into a small room with a single wooden table and two chairs. Jale was sitting alone inside, waiting for me to arrive. The lone guard followed me and, without saying a word, posted himself at the entrance door, his machine gun at ready! The second I looked at her, I could tell something was very wrong. I did not realize it was the sight of me that made her look so frightened. I sat down, leaning forward to hear her. She said in a deep whisper, "Michael, how are you?"

I sighed. Despite the look of concern and sadness on her face, it felt so good to talk with someone from the outside.

Jale understood that Buca Prison was a very bad place. She said she had heard many stories but knew of no American who had ever been held inside this evil place. She also sensed that my life was in danger if I could not get out. Her nervous small talk continued for a few minutes.

I abruptly stopped her and said in an impatient tone, "This is a bad place. I do not have much time. I am not interested in talking about how much tea I drink a day."

She looked a little embarrassed and began telling me that she had been in contact with Stephanie, my family, and my boss. She got the impression that some people high up in the American government were trying to help me.

"If I give you a letter," I asked, "could you get it to Stephanie?" She hesitated, but nodded, and told me to slide it under the table. She would hide it under her legs. The second I did this, the guard slowly walked over and said something in Turkish to Jale. She immediately got up, and he took the letter. I was devastated. She looked back at me sadly, not saying a word as she was escorted out.

7

A loud ruckus startled me awake in the middle of the night. Guards came down the block, banging on each cell door. I was cowering in the dark corner when they arrived at my cell. They opened the doors and forcefully ripped me from my cot. Dread welled up inside my stomach and throat. I was trotted down that infamous long, wet corridor and through a maze of old rooms until I got to the office, I had first been taken to when I arrived.

Inside, a small group of men stood behind another man who was seated at the only desk in the room. It was the same man I had met when I first arrived, the director of the prison. Also standing in the corner, almost hidden and appearing very timid, was Azra, my so-called lawyer. I was shocked to see her. A couple of months had passed since the last time I had seen her.

She discreetly motioned for me to lower my head and say nothing. I could tell she was very frightened, which frightened me even more. The shouting began. Lying in front of the director was my letter. The only words of English he spoke in his tirade were, "*No human rights!*" It was very evident my confiscated letter had struck a profoundly serious nerve with the Turkish prison authorities.

After he was finished, the director spoke to Azra and pointed at me. She came over and, in a serious tone I had not heard from her before, informed me that they were going to bring charges against me for defaming the state of Turkey. I would be brought before a tribunal and sentenced. As I was escorted out, I could not shake the look on Azra's face. It was etched upon my mind. For the first time it hit me that it was possible that I could spend a long, long time in this godforsaken place.

They did not take me back to my cell; instead, they dragged me back down through the prison maze and put me in isolation. I was in a dark, cold cell with no bunk or anything except a pile of wood that was used for the wood-burning stoves in the cellblocks.

This was the darkest period of my life. For whatever the explanation, I look back on this period and give definition to myself as "before" and "after" this time. In my worst nightmares, I could not have imagined such a place existed. That people existed who purposely depleted the human spirit to such a depth of despair.

I paced the dark corners of this cell, remembering people and events that had touched my life. I tried to think things through, looking at myself with all pretense stripped away. I experienced a whole range of emotions, and I went through each one, not being able to control my feelings. The terror of becoming one of those lost and forgotten souls existing within these wet walls turned to utter panic when I thought of my mother passing away and me not being able to see or speak to her again because I was rotting inside this hellhole. I am only now beginning to understand what had happened to me during those days. An evolution took place within me that was not some Zen-like philosophy or a born-again Christian brotherhood, but a deeply embedded anger.

God and I had never really been that close. I had never prayed before in times of need. When I tried talking to him, my thoughts and words for prayer felt awkward, and I felt slightly dishonest. Besides, I thought, *God did not really come into a place like this, he waited outside.* I spent hours sitting in the dark corner, my body so tense that I ached all over, expecting at any instant to be taken away for one of their infamous beatings. I lost control of the anger that built inside me. I hissed and spat out loud. I would endure the beatings and anything else they could throw at me. I had reached an extremely dangerous plateau where I was not afraid to be hurt. This became my demon for many years to come. My psyche went through a dramatic change during those dark days, and I understood I had gone to a place I had never experienced before in my life.

Huddled in the corner with my head down, I could hear Daoud's voice. I guessed he had been talking to me for several minutes. I struggled to come out of my fog and had never been happier to see anyone in my life. He was his usual witty self, but he carried a serious message. He told me the guards had been instructed to bring me nothing. He couldn't stay any longer and quickly handed me an old blanket and a small pot of che' (Turkish tea), along with a single loaf of bread. It was a feast. Nothing had ever tasted so good in my entire life.

Once a day for the next several days, his young boys would do the same. Each time, the boys would squat down outside the cell, and I would move over and sit next to them, talking in English, telling stories of where I came from. They smiled and nodded, not understanding anything I said. But they knew that human company was what I really needed. They took an enormous chance doing this; they saved me.

The last time I saw Daoud, he brought his che' and bread, along with a prison grapevine rumor that I would be leaving this place. Again, I could not help but wonder how this man managed to be in complete control in this godforsaken hole. The depth of his understanding and knowledge of human nature almost made him immune to the suffering and conditions around him. I also realized he and I had developed a bond. He knew I had to get out. He knew I would die in here if I stayed. My mentality would not allow me to adapt, and only later did I understand how much he had taught me.

I was extradited to Greece soon after.

8

My extraction from hell took almost two hours. The walk up that evil and menacing tunnel, with the Turkish inmates trying to see the American leaving through their cellblock doors, left an impression. This was an old place, the final stop for many. Faces of complete loss and despair, envy and excitement, cheered and shouted at me. Perhaps they hoped I might hold onto some part of their desperation. To them, I had become a member. I had spent time in the dungeon, maximum-security lockdown Buca Prison in Izmir, Turkey. I was one of the lucky ones: I walked out. They brought me into what they call their infirmary, which was really a musty old storage room with two chairs in the middle and all kinds of junk and garbage everwhere. With the guards' present, I stood in front of the so-called doctor. He was smoking one of those stinking Turkish cigarettes, the same ones that gave everyone in here permanently stained fingers. He wore street clothes that were right out of the '70s: polyester pants and a plaid shirt. I stared at the long ash barely hanging onto the cigarette in his mouth.

He gave me a quick glance and nodded, knocking off the ashes. This ended my examination. Every so often, a moment or a scene seemed so absurd that it would strike me in a comical way. This was one of those, and I think now that whatever mechanism in me did this helped me in the end.

I know I looked and smelled disgusting, but that came with this place. It included the guards and all personnel who worked inside. I was given a yellow sweater with buttons down the front, like something my grandpa used to wear. I learned the American

Consulate had sent it for me. I guess they were trying to spruce me up for the media.

I finally arrived at the all-too-familiar director's office. It was packed with people, mostly standing, but some were seated around the director's desk. The only people I recognized were from the American Consulate group and the ever-present Azra Immeler, my so-called lawyer, who had robbed me of about thirty-five thousand dollars. She knew how I felt toward her, so I am sure she was here for the publicity.

The American Consulate people included Randall Biggers, whom I had not seen since the first day of my arrest. Jale Kaptaner was also with him. Seeing Biggers again after what seemed like a lifetime ago made me react with a snarl and a slightly detectable hiss. He caught me glaring at him, standing in the middle of all these people, shackled and handcuffed.

After coming up out of that despicable, filthy dungeon of human squalor they called a prison, here I was thinking how ugly he appeared. I must have looked like some kind of caged animal to him. I was a completely different person than the one he had seen that first day seven months ago. I felt like a few lifetimes had passed since then.

He tried to smile at me, but he could not hide the startled look on his face, which quickly turned into fright at seeing my reaction. I thought about this moment much later, knowing I had been unable to mask my emotions.

After being in this place, I did not realize how I must have appeared to everyone. I was disoriented and in a slight fog after being inside for these past several months. I was nervous, but also relieved. A hard edge had crept into my persona, and I sensed I had become a curiosity to the people around me.

I noticed a subtle but distinct show of respect toward me by the prison officials and guards I encountered as I was led up through the dark, dingy corridors and through the huge steel gates as they loudly clanged open and then slammed shut behind me. Anyone who has served hard time knows that sound and the dread that comes with the closing of **Hell's Gates**.

I caught the eye of one of the crusty guards from down below. He gave me a sharp look and a quick nod. His look spoke volumes, but it was beyond my comprehension at the time. Thinking back, I know he was telling me to understand where I had been and what I had survived. His look cautioned me not to take this place home. It was an underground prison of lost souls and the *demons* that would follow, would destroy me if I let them. I felt a strange sense of pride to have survived. I thought anything would be easy from this point on. Little did I know how wrong I was.

An argument began between the Turkish officials and the two Greek marshals who had been sent for my extradition. From their body language and the few words of Turkish I had learned, I understood that the Turks wanted me shackled and handcuffed when I was escorted out the entrance where the media waited. The Greeks argued against it. This went on for quite a while. All of the sudden, a man standing in the back spoke, and everyone stopped shouting. He motioned for the guards to escort me to another office.

I met with him and two other men alone, and when he spoke perfect English, I was relieved. He was one of the bigwigs in the Turkish Interpol. That is why everyone paid attention to him. During the next half-hour, he summarized some things that absolutely shocked me. He gave me a brief account of how I had come to this. It was a long story that eventually ended up a tit-for-tat political game between Turkey and Greece, with a lot of crooks and cons in between. Despite what my lawyer and everyone else had said, there had never been a chance of me getting out of there until the Turkish state said so. It appeared to me that many players I did not know were involved in this mind-boggling escapade, and I had gotten caught in the middle.

The carnival-like atmosphere that accompanied my departure from the Turkish prison was nothing short of ridiculous, as every official and uniformed person wanted to be a part of it.

The two Greek marshals, along with a parade of Turkish police, escorted me to the Izmir airport in an old Turkish taxi. I think it was something like an old Chevy Impala with ripped seats. Small Turkish coffee cups, along with an ashtray full of Turkish cigarette butts, contributed to that stale smell that seemed to be everywhere. It was strange to be outside after so many months in the dark of those Turkish prisons. I was also nervous about being outside and moving forward, toward what I hoped would get this nightmare over with.

The two Greeks seemed almost proud that they were able to escort me without handcuffs. In their eyes, it was something to get one over on the Turks. I was just relieved not to have to wear that hardware for the trip to Athens. It was a huge procession to the airport. We were followed by newspaper reporters, cameramen, all the Turkish officials associated with the fiasco that had become my life and a lot who were not.

We arrived at the airport, and I found myself in the center of a parade of people as I was being led to a waiting room. The foreign media were shouting questions at me, but Turkish authorities refused to let me speak to them. It seemed like all the people at the airport turned toward me, pointing fingers and joining in this chaos. Of course, they recognized me from the front page of their newspapers over the last several months. Feeling they were witnessing something important; they joined the procession down the airport terminal.

Once again, I was relieved not to be wearing handcuffs on the flight to Athens. The two Greek marshals spoke fairly good English and appeared very relaxed with me. After the short flight from Izmir, still in somewhat of a fog and feeling unbalanced, I found myself in the Istanbul International Airport waiting for a connecting flight. I was having serious difficulty focusing after being underground in Buca Prison. I sat at a cafe table the Greeks had secured, looking around at the bustling chaos of these strange and foreign people. Suddenly, I realized I was alone.

Quickly, I glanced around and spotted the Greeks in line for another coffee. They were about twenty yards away and chatting with each other. Teeth clenched, I fought back the rush of adrenaline welling up in me. Frantically, the idea of escape came over me, and panic started to take over. I had thought of escape hundreds of times, dreamed about it, and tried to make a plan as to what I would do.

Suddenly, I realized this was my chance, probably my only chance. I struggled to formulate a plan. Looking around, I quickly studied the exits. I tried to visualize what I would do if I got outside the building. I had been to Istanbul a few times and knew the city a little. The grand bazaar, that is where I would hide. The largest outdoor bazaar in the world, it provided the confusion of hundreds of merchants and Turkish shoppers, mixed with the covered tents and the aromatic smell of exotic spices.

I thought this would provide a good cover until I could work things out and plan an escape inland to Ankara where the American Embassy was located.

As quickly as the thought of freedom possessed my senses, the fear of capture and the possibility of spending the rest of my life in the dungeon I had just left, locked behind *Hell's Gates*, snuffed out that fleeting moment. Striding toward me as if they could read my mind, the Greek marshals brought me back to the nightmare I was living. And I realized just how much it had already changed me.

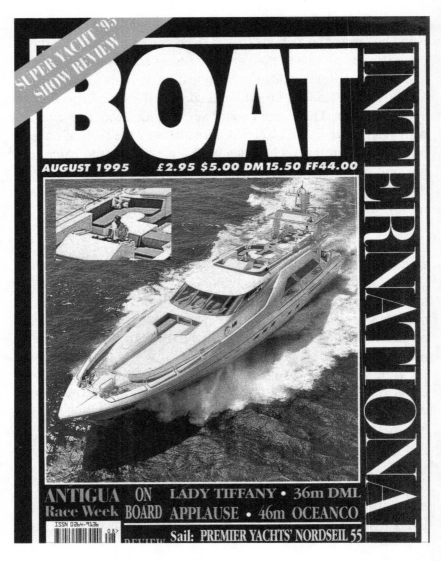

In 1995, Captain Churchward was at the top of his profession, his accomplishments had put him on the cover of Yacht and other magazines worldwide. Within two years his world would be turned upside down.

Captain Michael Churchward

THE WOOD REPORT

ISSUE 10   AUGUST/SEPTEMBER 1995

ON-BOARD COMMUNICATIONS SURVEY

M.Y. Lady Tiffany – New Vessel Report
Market Report – New Construction Information
Captain's Cruising Notes – The Panama Canal
Captain's Listing and Fuel Bunker Prices
New Product and Service Reviews

THE LEADING BUSINESS JOURNAL FOR THE CONSTRUCTION,
MANAGEMENT AND OPERATION OF LUXURY YACHTS

Captain Churchward 2000–2001.

Michael and his mother after his return home.

Michael's family all came to Florida after he got home. First time in almost 30 years his mother had all her children together.

Mike Churchward expresses his feelings after a 35-0 win over Tustin.
Mike Churchward-All-League Team, All-County Team,
All-League Back of the Year,
All-County Back of the Year,
Most Valuable Player

Michael in high school playing football, growing up an all-American kid in
Orange, California, 1971. (Smaller picture is senior yearbook photo.)

Michael with his oldest and dearest friend Brad Williams at a high school reunion. I learned to cherish those lifelong friendships that sustained through the years, regardless of the different paths' life had taken us.

Michael and his crew, Turkey '97, two weeks before arrest.

Dustin Hoffman with Michael on board *Picante.*

Amerikalı kaptan Söke'de hapis

Olayı duyar duymaz hemen Kuşadası'na gelen Kaptan'ın nişanlısı Stephanie Morr, '- Türk adaletine güveniyorum" diyor.

Kaptan Churcward, Dustin Hoffman ile Brad Pitt'i, bu yatla Ege kıyılarında dolaştırdı.

Yunanlı armatörün suçlamaları sonucu Atina'da hakkında mahkumiyet kararı verilen Kaptan Churward, 60 gündür tutuklu

1991 yılında Yunanlı armatör Stylianos Harakaglov'un özel yatını kullanan Amerikalı Kaptan Churcward, tekneyi Karaipler'e götürürken, Malta açıklarında motor arızasıyla karşılaştı. Önce çevreden yardım isteyen kaptan, sonra tekneyi Tunus'a götürmeyi başardı. Harakaglov'un teknesi Tunus'ta tamir edildi ama yapılan masrafları sigortadan alamayan Yunanlı armatör ile kaptan Churward arasında anlaşmazlık çıktı.

Atina'da mahkum oldu

Yunanlı'nın kendisini suçlaması üzerine teknenin anahtarlarını fırlatıp atan kaptan, ekibi ile birlikte topluca işi bıraktı. Ancak Harakaglov hırsızlık suçlamasıyla Kaptan'dan davacı olup, onu Atina'da bir mahkemede mahkum ettirdi. Aradan geçen 7 yıl boyunca sayısız teknede görev yapan Kaptan, gelişmelerden habersiz, dünyaca ünlü isimleri Ege ve Akdeniz kıyılarında dolaştırdı.

Yunan Adalarına defalarca gitti

Bu süre içinde Yunan adalarına defalarca giriş-çıkış yapan Kaptan Churcward'ı izleyen Armatör Harakaglov, onun için Türk polisine Interpol emrini ulaştırıp Kuşadası'nda yakalanmasını sağladı. Yunanistan'a iadesi istenen Kaptan için kararı Adalet Bakanlığı verecek. **SAYFA 11'DE**

Bu ekip "hırsızlıkla" suçlanıyor Yunanlı armatör, hepsi iyi eğitim almış, pek çok sanatçı ve işadamını güvenle denizlerde dolaştırmış olan Churcward ve arkadaşlarını, hırsızlıkla suçluyor. Kaptanın Türkiye'de yakalanmasının aleyhimize propaganda malzemesi haline gelmesinden korkuyor.

Turkish newspaper headlines.

61

Kaptan iade ediliyor

Atina mahkemelerinin gıyabında verdiği karar nedeniyle Kuşadası'nda tutuklanıp 4 aydır Söke Cezaevi'nde yatan Amerikalı Kaptan için, Bakanlar Kurulu'ndan karar çıktı

7 yıl önce, teknesini kullandığı Yunanlı bir armatörle anlaşmazlığa düşüp ekibiyle işi bırakan; bunu hazmedemeyen armatörün gıyabında açtığı ve yürüttüğü davadan haberdar olmayıp Kuşadası'nda tutuklanan Kaptan Churchward için kötü haber var: Atina'da kendisini savunma fırsatı bile bulamadığı için Türkiye'de yargılanmak isteyen Amerikalı Kaptan'ın isteği kabul edilmedi.

Uluslararası anlaşmalara göre

Söke Asliye Hukuk Mahkemesi'nin verdiği "uluslararası anlaşma ve hukuk kuralları nedeniyle Kaptan'ın iade edilmesi" kararı, Bakanlar Kurulu tarafından da imzalanıp Cumhurbaşkanı Demirel'e gönderildi. Kararı Demirel'in de onaylaması üzerine

Ünlü sanatçı Dustin Hoffman başta olmak üzere, pek çok ünlünün yatını kullanan Kaptan Churchward, işi bıraktığı için kızdırdığı Yunanlı armatörün hışmına uğradı. Tek suçu, hakkını yeterince aramamak olan Kaptan için ünlüler, Türkiye ve Yunanistan'ı faks yağ-

Amerikalı kaptan Söke'de hapis

Captain Churchward and Stephanie were on the front page of the Turkish newspapers for months.

God Waits Outside

Kandil gecesi camiyi soydular

ANKARA - Maltepe Camii'nin bağış kutusu, Miraç dili'nin kutlandığı gece çalındı. Olay yerinde yapılan İncelemede, hırsız ya da hırsızların, caminin dış kapısını yarak ana kapıya ulaştıkları, daha sonra da camı kı içinde yaklaşık 2 milyon lira bulunan bağış kutusunı rinden söktükleri belirlendi.

Amerikalı
iade e

Taksi şoförü Hüseyin Güven (sağda) parayı sahibine teslim etmenin, Ziya Sevim (solda) ise parasına kavuşmanın sevincini yaşadı.

Örnek
davranış

İSTANBUL- Atatürk Hava Limanı'ndan aldığı bir yolcunun takside unuttuğu 13 bin 30 mark ve 10 guldeni (Yaklaşık birbuçuk milyar) hiç tereddüt etmeden sahibine teslim eden taksi şoförü Hüseyin Güven büyük takdir topladı.

Önceki gece yarısı saat: 23.00 sıralarında havalimanından aldığı Ziya Sevim'i Bahçelievler'deki evine götüren taksi şoförü Hüseyin Güven dönüşte araçta unutulan çantayı farke-

Gitmek istemiyor Söke Kapalı Cezaevi'nde dört aydır tutuklu bulunan Amerikalı kaptan Michael Chucward, Yunanistan'a iade edilecek

SÖKE (İHA) - Söke Kapalı Cezaevi'nde dört aydır tutuklu bulunan Amerikalı kaptan Michael Chucward, Yunanistan'ın başvurusu üzerine bu ülkeye iade ediliyor. Yunanlı armatör Sitilaus ile tartışarak işi bırakan Amerikalı kaptan, suçladığı Yunanlı patronu tarafından Atina'da mahkemeye verilmiş, arandığı sırada geldiği Kuşadası Limanı'nda gemisinden alınarak tutuklanmıştı. Chucward'ın iade kararı Bakanlar Kurulu'ndan sonra Cumhurbaşkanı tarafından da imzalandı.

Atina 16. Olağan Mahkemesi'nin gıyabında verdiği mahkûmiyet kararı sebebiyle "hırsızlık" suçlamaları ile karşı karşıya kalan Chucward, Yunanistan ile Türkiye arasında yürürlükte olan "suçluların iadesi" anlaşmasına binaen Avrupa Sözleşmesi hükümlerince su-

Turkish newspaper headlines, Michael being transferred prisons.

63

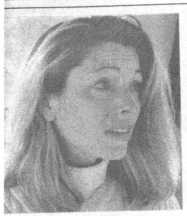

Mutsuzluğun gözyaşları!

67 gündür Söke Cezaevi'nde yatan Amerikalı Kaptan Churchward'ın tahliye isteği reddedildi

Kaptan Churchward'ın avukatı Azra İnmeler'ın Aydın Ağır Ceza Mahkemesi'ne yaptığı "tahliye başvurusunun" reddedilmesi üzerine, umutsuzluğa kapılan nişanlısı Stephanie Morr ağlamaya başladı. Avukat İnmeler, "Kararı yazılı emirle bozdurmak için Yargıtay Cumhuriyet Başsavcılığı'na başvuracağız" dedi.　　**11'DE**

Kaptan Churchward

Stephanie Morr, nişanlısının tahliye talebinin reddedildiğini öğrenince gözyaşlarını tutamadı.

Stephanie outside Soke Prison when she was told I would not be released.

The Herald

Broward Final

www.herald.com

THE BROWARD EDITION OF THE MIAMI HERALD

SUNDAY, NOVEMBER 16, 1997 　　　BRO　　　75 Cents
For home delivery, call 954-462-3000

Dream life dissolving into Turkish nightmare

By DAVID KIDWELL
Herald Staff Writer

Michael Churchward is entrusted with multi-million dollar yachts, hundreds of thousands of dollars in cash and the lives of his crew and well-heeled passengers over months on rough seas.

He's never swiped so much as a Waterford crystal goblet or a Limoges china plate.

But Churchward's life of wipe, caviar and leather settees — his promising career as captain to scores

An American yacht captain sits in a foreign prison while his fiance in Fort Lauderdale explores every avenue to try to free him.

of wealthy industrialists and such celebrities as Dustin Hoffman — has been interrupted by a stay in a rat-infested Turkish prison cell flooded

with human sewage.

Churchward, 44, was imprisoned in Soke on July 20 because of a 6-year-old dispute with a former boss, a Greek shipping tycoon who says Churchward and his crew tried to steal an 85-foot sailing yacht.

To many, the allegation is befuddling and implausible.

"The whole idea is ludicrous, not only to people who know Michael, but to anyone who has any knowledge

PLEASE SEE PRISON, 18A　　Churchward

Miami Herald front page.

(10/6)

DEAR STEPH,   SAT. NOV. 30, 1997

WHAT IS HAPPENING TO ME NOW IS BEYOND WORDS.
I'M IN A CELL BLOCK WITH ALL THE IRAQIS + IRANIANS,
→ PAKISTANIS, ECT. WHO FOR VARIOUS REASONS ARE WAITING
FOR THE TURKISH COURTS TO DECIDE OUR FATE. ITS
UNBELIEVABLE, THERE IS ONLY ONE WAY TO DESCRIBE THE
CONDITIONS. "DEATH ROW!" THERE ARE NO HUMAN RTS HERE
IN TURKEY. SOME OF THESE PEOPLE HAVE BEEN WAITING FOR
A COURT DATE FOR MONTHS + MONTHS. A COUPLE EVEN YEARS.
THE LIVING SITUATION IS SOMETHING I WILL HAVE TO WAIT
TO TELL YOU. I DARE NOT WRITE IT DOWN. THIS IS A
FREE FOR ALL, YOU EAT IF YOU HAVE RESOURCES, IF YOU DON'T
YOU GO HUNGRY OR ARE AT THE MERCY OF SOMEONE ELSE.
(DO YOU KNOW WHAT I MEAN)! I AM IN A CELL 5' x 10'
WITH 2 OTHER PEOPLE, NOTHING ELSE BUT A HOLE IN THE
FLOOR TO SHIT IN, IT DOESN'T FLUSH SO YOU HAVE TO GO GET
A BUCKET OF WATER EVERYTIME. I WONT DISCUSS CONDITIONS
ANYMORE. (I ESPECIALLY DON'T WANT YOU TO WORRY, I CAN
SURVIVE (AND THATS ALL I'M DOING) I HAVE LEARNED SOME
INCREDIBLE THINGS THAT YOU HAVE TO PAY ATTENTION TO.
BECAUSE I COULD HAVE BEEN OUT LONG AGO IF WE KNEW HOW
TO DO IT, THE SAME SITUATION APPLIES TO GREECE.
(EVEN MORE SO) I NEED A GREEK LAWYER WHO CAN BROKER
A DEAL WITH THE PROS. THATS THE ONLY WAY TO DO THIS
QUICKLY. OUR MISTAKE HERE WAS NOT HAVING A
LAWYER-/ BROKER THATS HOW IT WORKS FOR FOREIGNERS.
IF YOU ALLOW ME TO GET CAUGHT UP THE THE SYSTEM
LIKE ACRA DID (I'M DEAD) PLEASE TRY TO UNDERSTAND
THIS!
    PS. PLEASE GIVE THIS TO MR.

(left margin, vertical:) PURE + COMPLETE SS$OR! RUSSIANS

(left margin, vertical:) X THERE ARE 2000 PRISONERS HERE!

Captain Churchward's confiscated letter that got him thrown into solitary
confinement. He mentioned "No Human Rights."

65

Churchward Kept in Solitary Confinement

On December 12th 1997 Michael Churchward was extradited to Athens, Greece from Ismir, Turkey where he spent his final days in solitary confinement.

Churchward's final month in Turkey was by far the worst of his incarceration since July 20th, 1997, when he was taken into custody by Turkish authorities on Interpol charges of allegedly stealing a 85 foot sailing vessel some seven years ago from a Greek businessman, a previous employer of Churchward's. From the start, circumstances leading to and after he was taken by Turkish authorities have lead many to believe he is being victimized unjustly by the former employer and that the charges have been fabricated.

It appears that the Turkish prison and those who are in control did not take too kindly of the description of conditions at the prison in an article published several weeks ago by the Miami Herald. Was it the 20 men to a single cell left to defecate in a hole in the center of the room, or perhaps intermittent water that was supplied or maybe the fact that Churchward was getting used to the four legged rodents that sometimes would share the cell. Whatever ruffled the Turks feathers was enough to keep him cold in the harsh winter, verbally threatened and finally placed in solitary confinement for his final days in Turkey.

Today Churchward is in "a prison in Athens thereby conditions have improved as far as prisons go and he has been in contact with his family and fiancé Stephanie Moore. The move to Greece from where the charges were lodged has started a new process with a different government. New laws, new attorneys, new rules and new expenses."

As for the defense of Michael Churchward the wheels are turning, slowly, but they are turning. The expenses of fighting a

Churchward kept in solitary confinement *Miami Herald* article.

Churchward's Nightmare Continues in Turkey!

For Michael Churchward, his family and fiancee Stephanie Moor the past 150 days have been nothing short of a nightmare.

Michael Churchward, 44, was the Captain on the yacht "Picante" for several years traveling the world for his owner Philip Restino and charter guests such as Dustin Hoffman. That was until July 20th when Churchward's life was turned upside down by a stay in not one, but two Turkish prisons, where he remains today.

Churchward, was imprisoned first in Soke on July 20th on charges that he and (former) crew, tried to steal a 85-foot sailing yacht, a car, and belongings from a former Greek boss with a shady past some 7 years ago.

Stephanie Morr & Micheal Churchward

As Churchward survives in a country in which he had brought guests of "Picante" for vacations, his fiancee and family sift the way through the maze of politics and bureaucrats looking for cash with worthless guarantees. From cash being handed to those who say they can get him out in one breath, to saying they can make sure he never leaves Turkey in the other. From having to find a guard in the prison to pass notes, and having to pay someone to get a blanket to Michael during Turkey's cold winter are just some of the basic challenges they face.

Today Michael sits in a prison in Ismir, Turkey with no contact whatsoever. Stephanie has not received a letter from Michael weeks and the only assurance of his existance is from the US Embassy. US officials are watching the Turks and pushing them to play by their own rules, since it is still unclear what really happened seven years ago between Churchward and former Harkoglou. Many believe that the whole thing was fabricated.

They have lost everything trying to get Michael out and things do not look promising. Extradition papers have been signed, Churchward's extradition to Greece where he could sit for years until his case is heard.

Efforts are on going daily, from our Congressman here in South Florida, to Ross Perot, who has taken an interest in Churchward's well being, to the yacht management company BSA which handled "Picante". The international yachting community is up in arms. Captains and owners are calling to out of Turkey and Greece, which are very popular summer cruising spots for the Mega-yachts, but no more.

M/Y "Picante's" Crew, better days in Marmauis, Turkey.
Marcus Ryan David Rutherford Michael Churchward Miles Pur
Stephanie Morr Charlie Walker

E. CLAY SHAW
22o DISTRICT, FLORIDA

2408 RAYBURN HOUSE OFFICE BUILDING
WASHINGTON, DC 20515
(202) 225-3026

DISTRICT OFFICES:
BROWARD COUNTY
1512 EAST BROWARD BOULEVARD
SUITE 101
FORT LAUDERDALE, FL 33301
(954) 522-1800

PALM BEACH COUNTY
222 LAKEVIEW AVENUE, #162
WEST PALM BEACH, FL 33401
(561) 832-2007

DADE & PALM BEACH COUNTIES
TOLL FREE
800-7420

COMMITTEE:
WAYS AND MEANS
SUBCOMMITTEES:
CHAIRMAN
HUMAN RESOURCES
TRADE

CHAIRMAN
FLORIDA CONGRESSIONAL DELEGATION

Congress of the United States
House of Representatives
Washington, DC 20515–0922

March 9, 1998

Mr. R. Nicholas Burns, United States Ambassador
United States Embassy
Athens, Greece
PSC 108, APO AE 09842

Dear Mr. Ambassador:

This is in further reference to my constituent, Michael Churchward, who is currently being held in Korydallos Prison in Athens. It is my understanding that Mr Churchward's trial has been set for April 1, 1998, and I want to make you aware of the strong support that exists for Mr. Churchward here in South Florida.

Fort Lauderdale, Florida harbors an international yachting community that is unparalleled in the United States. Because I was unacquainted with Mr. Churchward prior to his difficulties, I made many inquiries in that community regarding his situation, job history, character and reputation. Without exception, the reply was that Mr. Churchward had the loftiest standards and personal ethics, and that he would be hired in positions of the greatest responsibility with no qualms whatsoever. Indeed, I received dozens of letters of recommendations, unsolicited.

As you can see from the enclosed *Miami Herald* article, this case is highly visible in South Florida. There is little doubt that the outcome of the trial, and the fairness of the verdict will be widely reported. While I understand that you must allow the Greek government to operate within their own rule of law, I very much hope you will provide the highest appropriate level of support to Mr. Churchward and his family.

As you suggested in our telephone conversation, I will be in contact with Greece's Ambassador to the United States. Thank you for any assistance you might give to Mr. Churchward.

Sincerely,

E. Clay Shaw, Jr.
Member of Congress

THIS STATIONERY PRINTED ON PAPER MADE OF RECYCLED FIBERS

One of many letters written by congressmen.
This one is from Congressman E. Clay Shaw.

9

The plane arrived at Athens International Airport in the middle of the night. I was the first one off the plane, escorted through a dark, freezing rain to a waiting police van, which took me to a remote part of the airport. The Greek Interpol marshals handed me over to four uniformed policemen, and I was briskly ushered through a makeshift custom station without a passport check to another police van outside.

The loneliness hit me hard. I had already learned that a man's mental anguish can be accompanied by physical pain. I understood this with every fiber of my body. My journey was taking its toll on my inner as well as my outer strength. Had I reached my emotional limits? I could not allow that, knowing there would still be so much more to endure.

It would be so easy to slip into that vast dark space where a person's mind can hide from utter despair. I had seen other men go there just so they could survive. The progression was recognizable: they let themselves become dirty and unkempt, shuffling along in a zombie-like manner with a glazed, empty look in their eyes. These were the telltale signs they had given up. "Keep fighting. Just keep fighting, Michael!" I silently repeated to myself. Another foreign country, another foreign prison where everyone spoke another foreign language. Held prisoner for something I did not do. Not knowing what the future holds, not knowing if and when I would get a trial. Not even knowing if my family knew where I was or what was happening to me.

They say it takes two years to get to a Greek court. The thought of spending more years in a foreign prison just to get to a court was something I could not bring myself to think about. I knew I had lost everything, but none of that mattered to me now. I just needed to get home.

The isolation of Buca Prison, the hostile foreign environment, and not being able to understand the language was a huge stress I had lived with every minute of every day. I was not sure my mental and physical strength would last. I was not sure I had anything left.

That first night, I was taken from the airport to a local jail and kept in a holding tank. It was pitch black when they opened the cell door. I could hear men at the back of the cell but could not see anyone. I stood by the locked gate holding my small sack of belongings. I could have fallen asleep standing up, but I forced myself to keep my eyes open until I could get a feel of what was around me. I was not afraid, and I realized that my time in the Turkish prisons had hardened me.

It seemed like I had just closed my eyes when I was awakened by loud voices. I was shocked by the number of men inside the cell. At least twenty men were all shouting about something as sunlight filtered in through the front of the cell. I noticed an immediate difference between the Turks and the Greeks: the Greeks were a much louder people. In fact, they did not speak; they shouted constantly.

The gritty, nasty feeling had become almost routine. No shower, no clean clothes, not being able to brush my teeth. These were thoughts that rarely crossed my mind, except for today. I would have given anything to be able to clean myself.

By mid-day, I thought I had been forgotten when suddenly a group of men appeared. They were wearing suits and talking among themselves. The jailer motioned for me to step up to the gate. The group turned to look at me with obvious interest. One man stepped forward and introduced himself as a lawyer in Athens. He said my boss, Mr. R., had sent him. He quickly passed his hand through the cell bars and handed me some drachma (Greek money). He spoke English and told me that certain people would be in contact once I was settled in Korydallos Prison.

His reassurance filled me with confidence and hope, and I vigorously shook his hand and thanked him. I was not alone.

Korydallos Prison in Athens was a maximum-security lockdown with about eighteen hundred inmates who were housed in four cellblocks. The conditions were better than Turkey, but I was soon to learn that, in many ways, it was a far more dangerous place.

We were brought into the compound and entered a group of offices to start the processing. The place was crowded, everyone shouting at each other in Greek. Of course, I could not understand the language. When they escorted me to the front of the line, it felt like I was expected.

A mysterious small man appeared at my side and whispered sternly for me to ask for cellblock B. He spoke with an Australian accent and said he was part of an organization. An inmate named Lefteri would make contact, he said. He handed me a pair of Levis and tennis shoes and quickly disappeared.

I wondered who the hell he was and what was going on. He must have had some kind of clout to get near me. Things had started out bizarre and were getting even more so. Cellblock B was a three-story enclosure with cells on each side that looked down a wide cement corridor. It housed about four hundred inmates, many of them doing life.

With my bedroll and belongings under my arm, the lockdown was opened, and I entered Block B. The noise was deafening. Men were all over the place, standing in groups, scheming, and socializing. I felt the eyes of several cons checking me out. I was not conscious of the impression I gave, but I knew, on looking back, it was not apprehension or shyness. After being in the Turkish prison system, something automatically emanates from you, and it is not softness. I heard a loud shout from the other end of the block: "Hey Amerikani!" At least I am being welcomed, I thought sarcastically.

I found my cell on the third floor. I was anxious about entering an unfamiliar living space, and when I stepped in, I was greeted by a group of men huddled together. They all turned to look at me, but no one spoke. A small guy motioned for me to take the top bunk, and that was that. This was now my third prison and second foreign country. It had been a long time since I had felt good or had a simple, happy thought. That, in itself, was difficult to live with.

It was funny, but I actually missed Daoud and his boys back in the dungeon. Still, I was determined to put that experience out of my mind and move forward. Staying to myself, I roamed around the third floor in cellblock B. When night lockdown came, I went back to my cell.

Right away, I noticed someone had gone through my things. Everything had been stolen: my new jeans, tennis shoes, watch... anything of value. My cellmate avoided my glare and said nothing. I felt my blood boil, but I was disgusted with myself for being so careless. I knew I needed to sharpen my wits. This was a whole different place, and I had to get in the game.

I opened my eyes after a restless sleep and found myself in the darkness of yet another strange place. I could make out the silhouette of my cellmate. He had a strap around his upper arm and was frantically probing for a fresh place to stick a soiled needle. Lying there, I realized my things had been stolen to pay for his heroin habit. This was just great. My first cellmate was a *lazacki*, Greek slang for junkie. I closed my eyes, stifling a small sob, and felt a little sorry for myself. I wondered what had happened to my life, and if I would ever find the way out of this labyrinth.

Over the next few days, I got to know the cellblock routine, who was who, and where things were. We were allowed out into a large dirt area for one-hour mid-morning and another hour mid-afternoon. The cells were open to the cellblock for much of the day.

I was roaming around on the main corridor when a small man with a smile and a kind face introduced himself as Mario. He was Italian and spoke English well. He talked non-stop, and I realized he knew who I was. I liked him immediately and enjoyed the conversation.

Mario was a bit of a gossip and seemed to know all about everyone, including me. He had gotten fifteen years for associating with drug dealers. Three of those years had passed. The thought that he had twelve more to go made me shudder all the way through. He was from Milan, Italy, and sold clothing and fabrics to merchants in Athens. I did not really care why he was here, or whether he was guilty or not, but I did appreciate the company.

Suddenly, I noticed a man walking toward me with my watch on. Without thinking, I blurted out, "Hey, that's my watch!"

I felt a hand grip my arm and Mario hissed, "Are you crazy? He's Albanian. Forget about the watch." He quietly explained that Albanian gangs controlled many things in Korydallos, including the drug trade and the highly valued telephones for which a phone card had to be purchased.

There were only five pay phones for the four hundred people inside. It was a valuable commodity, and the Albanians guarded them with diligence. The Albanians were easy to spot dark-skinned, smaller men who always traveled in packs. They never confronted a victim one on one but attacked viciously in gangs.

Mario's voice took on a venomous tone as he explained that these people had flooded across the Albanian-Greek border when the Cold War ended. Albania was one of the most repressed countries in the world. They had gone generations without education and knew nothing of the simple principles of human respect. They had no idea what the word meant and certainly had none for other people or for themselves. They were animals, and they were extremely dangerous. He cautioned me to avoid them at all costs.

A few days later, I witnessed the ruthlessness of these people for myself. I was in the back of a long line for the phones when a quick-moving swarm of Albanians attacked an old Greek man without mercy. They were relentless in their beating, breaking his face with their boots. Everyone scattered, nobody daring to stop them. I could not move, watching the viciousness of their attack. The old man's bones were cracking, blood gushing from the gashes in his head. To witness men beating other men without any restraint or boundaries is sickening.

The sounds of fists and boots meeting bones, along with the agonizing wail of the old man pleading for help, wrenched my guts.

After Mario's warning, and the reality before me, it would be a huge mistake to intervene. I could feel my fists tighten, as I started to boil over with anger. Without thinking, I stepped forward, but out of nowhere, I was forcefully shoved from the side. I turned, ready to defend myself, facing a thick man a little taller than me.

The intensity in his voice stopped me in my tracks. "I am Lefteri," he said. "You have many things to learn in here if you want to live. Follow me!"

He cleared a path through the melee, and I instantly understood that Lefteri was a guy I did not want to mess with. Physically, he was not overpowering—about six feet tall with a strong upper body, in his early forties—but he had a presence that made you hesitate and take notice. Later, I learned he had the respect of inmates and guards alike. I noticed even the loudest and most obnoxious of men seemed to lose their voices when he was around.

I followed him to his cell, and soon learned he was the only man in the block who lived alone. His cell was like a tiny studio apartment, where he had made himself amazingly comfortable. His job in the prison was running the compound computers. This had earned him chief trustee status, enabling him to come and go easily. He told me he had been asked to look after me and help if he could. I wanted to know who had asked him to help me and where all this good will had originated.

He snapped back, "That might come later; for now, just keep your head down and learn the system."

He was sharp and straight to the point. I got the idea he was not going to babysit me, but if I needed something, I only had to ask. I told him about my cellmate, and that I was worried about getting in trouble being around the drugs.

To this, he only shrugged. "I will get your case papers, get familiar, and help you make a plan." His tone was ominous as he added, "I will not help if you are going to be stupid. Do not involve yourself with other disputes, and do not try to be so tough. It will only get you hurt...and stay clear of the Albanians!"

I stiffened, fists clenched, thinking if he only knew where I had just come from. His stare caught my eyes, and I was unable to look away.

Reading my mind, he said, "It doesn't matter where you came from; it only matters that you are here." He turned away, and I saw that I had been dismissed. I left his cell more confused than I had been before.

My new friend, Mario, was hanging out not far from Lefteri's cell. He seemed excited, and he and his two friends waved me over. They looked like munchkins, making the same movements in unison.

Mario spoke quickly, his arms gesturing with every sentence. "I can't believe what I see! You and Lefteri!" He was almost spitting on himself in his excitement. "No one gets invited inside his cell! How do you know him?" he asked.

I muttered something noncommittal, and he rambled on. "What did you talk about? Can you introduce me?"

I stepped back, smiling at him, and asked why he wanted to know all this. I was still a little cautious of everyone and did not want to say too much.

Mario almost hissed as he said, "Do you know who he is?" Without waiting for my answer, he continued, "Lefteri is the main man in here. He can do favors, big favors!" Mario had been inside three years; and the idea of meeting or talking with Lefteri made him very hyper.

I was beginning to understand the inmate structure and realized I had just gotten very lucky. Later, I would learn Lefteri had a lot more clout than any of these guys knew.

My first week in Korydallos Prison was a blur. I had trouble focusing. The complete change of environment, language, and culture had me off balance. The constant pressure of looking over my shoulder for anything or anyone coming at me was a fact of life in this place, and it never let up.

During the following days, I managed to use the telephone. I was able to buy a phone card at the prison canteen, where I found that several drachmas had been mysteriously deposited for me. I had to wait in line an hour and a half for the phone, and you were only allowed two minutes, enforced by the Albanians, but I finally reached one of the phones mounted on the wall.

I was sweaty with nerves and my hands shook as I finally picked up the receiver. The wait in line—where anything could and often did happen, and the fact that it was my first time using a phone in many months—made me feel like everyone was watching. I feared I would misdial the long-distance number to Florida and have to start all over again.

I had not spoken to Stephanie for months and had no idea what was happening at home. The ringing went on and on. If she wasn't home, I knew it would hit me hard. But then, I heard her soft hello on the other side, ten thousand miles away. My eyes filled with tears. I had my arm over my head, my face against the wall, trying to hide my conversation from the other inmates. I could barely hear her, and I only had two minutes. I managed to say I was okay and would try to call again tomorrow.

When I hung up, I noticed Mario and his munchkins hovering close by. Seeing the emotion in my eyes brought a sad look to his face and stopped him from approaching. I quickly walked away, thinking I did not want to appear vulnerable and certainly did not want to share any of my personal business with anyone. This had been my code since the beginning of my ordeal, and I needed to stick to it.

10

The days and weeks passed painfully slow. Christmas day came, and with it came depression and self-reflection. The worst was the flood of self-pity I could not fight off. I stood alone outside my cell and looked at the huge lockup, not really seeing it. After several minutes of missing my family and the people I loved, I decided to go look for my friend Mario.

I found him and his ever-present sidekicks down on the main corridor. "More festive this morning," I said casually as I looked around.

"It's a busy visitor's day for the Greeks and their families," he replied. "Wait to you see what happens next."

Suddenly, without notice, everyone was moving. Men from the second and third floors were coming downstairs, filling the main corridor. There was a big commotion down at the cellblock gates. I could not see what was happening, but I could hear it. The loud chanting of the Greek priests rose above the excited hum of the inmates. The procession was coming down the corridor, and when I was able to see what was going on, I turned to Mario and said, "You got to be kidding me!"

He just smiled with an I-told-you-so look.

The high priest was a huge man with a long white beard, dressed in a colorful religious frock. He was seated on a Roman-like throne that was carried by eight other priests. A few lesser priests were swinging brass urns spewing clouds of incense that filled the cellblock. But the real show was watching these hardened men throw themselves at the feet of the high priest, desperately trying to kiss an outstretched hand sporting an enormous ruby ring.

For a few moments I shared a smile with Mario as we watched the spectacle. Then, thinking how very far from home I was, that awful homesick feeling came over me.

After the show, Mario told me he was going to the prison chapel for Mass and suggested I go with him. Inmates were allowed to do this in controlled groups at different times throughout the day. Today, it was standing room only in the small church, and we were packed in shoulder-to-shoulder. The non-stop wailing of the Greek priest singing prayers and the thick cloud of incense in the room made me wish I had missed this.

Mario nudged me, wanting me to look up and see what was making him laugh. To the side and in front of us was an inmate with a skinhead. Tattooed on the back of his head were the large numbers "666." I had all I could do to keep from bursting out laughing. Mario continued making faces and crossing his fingers like crucifixes, trying to make me lose it.

Later that night, after lockdown, I lay in my bunk, self-pity descending on me like a dark cloud. I thought about how alien everything felt, and I desperately wanted to be home on this *Christmas night, 1997.*

Eventually, I did get transferred out of the cell with the *lazacki*, although my new cell was just as dreadful. I shared my new quarters with a Greek orthodox priest who had murdered his wife, spoke no English, and was filthy. Worst of all, in his sleep, every imaginable disgusting sound came out of his body. I felt like I was living in a barn with farm animals. Some nights I would lay sleepless, anticipating the vulgar noises, when suddenly some sort of explosion would erupt from him, shaking the bunks. The man was revolting, but I had not been offered a choice. I had never seen anything like it. Sleep was minimal. Even if I were to beat the hell out of him, it would make no difference.

These were tough days. The lack of sleep and constant anxiety over the violence in the prison made me aggressive and impatient about the lack of progress on my case and uncertainty and not knowing what would happen to me. I felt everything in my life slipping away. I realized the cellmate or mates you got stuck with could make all the difference in how you did your time.

Unfortunately, I never had a good cellmate my entire time in Korydallos. All that could be said about it was that it was better than the isolation and squalor of Buca Prison in Turkey.

A court date had not been set for my trial, and the stories I heard inside were frightening. The average time to get a trial date was about two years. There was no such thing as bail, and due process was nonexistent. You endured the lockdown until they got around to you; or you tried to find other ways out. Sentences handed out were so lopsided in relation to the crime; it was normal to get double-digit years for the simplest of offenses. I was told that given the charges against me, I could expect at least twenty to thirty years. *Even if I was innocent!* I screamed inside when I heard this. My mental state did back flips; I just refused to accept it.

I tried to talk to anyone who could give me solid, useful information. The language barrier was so difficult to overcome that it just multiplied my stress and anxiety. I knew that if you were a foreigner, money decided the number of years you would do, and I became obsessed with navigating the way out of my own personal labyrinth.

The system, I realized, was so completely corrupt that it was critical to find the right people to pay in order to make things work. My frustration even extended to Stephanie, family, and some friends, who kept saying these people could not do this to me.

I was inside these hideous prison walls, living it every day, so obviously they could do it to me. I realized that people on the outside could not begin to understand what I was experiencing. They were unable to comprehend, and I could not possibly begin to explain, the isolation or the constant fear interspersed with moments of pure terror. I could not expect them to understand the loss of hope, the deadening of feeling, the paranoia. Only another person who has done hard time in a foreign place could maybe understand what prisons like these were like.

I had struggled to survive the prison system in Turkey and now in Greece without due process and under a mandate that finds you guilty until proven innocent. The diabolical corruption of these systems was fueled by their complete disorganization and their absolute disregard for human concerns. Lives were lost and the lost forgotten because of nothing more than an illogical or malicious decision by a lower bureaucrat with a uniform. Many of my supporters at home were incapable of digesting the fact that such a system really existed.

I have always been patriotic—a red, white, and blue type guy. Having lived and experienced such an abuse of individual rights gave me a much better understanding of exactly what America is. It taught me a huge respect and love for the United States. I *ached* to get home.

11

Having managed to get through the worst Christmas of my life, it was well into the New Year and nothing had changed for me. Lefteri got me transferred to another cell on the ground floor with a little Japanese man, a merchant seaman who had stabbed his first officer on a drunken shore leave. He had been sentenced to forty-five years. My situation was better (at least I could get a little sleep), although the little Jap was a whack job. Later, he was to become a dangerous whack job.

My new cell put me right next door to probably the most infamous inmate in Korydallos Prison. Yianni was a young Greek in his early twenties. He had movie star looks and a quick, friendly smile. Well educated, he spoke perfect English, and his gregarious personality and enthusiasm made me like him immediately. He knew who I was, because he was one of the few guys in here who had access to Lefteri, and he had been told a few things about me. He worked in the prison canteen and went out of his way to make sure I was able to get what I needed from whatever limited items were available.

After we got to know each other, he became eager to tell me his story. His trial had been front-page news in the Greek newspapers well before I had arrived. At the young age of twenty, he had been found guilty of murder, and he was going to be in this place for the rest of his natural life. He had come from a prosperous Greek family that had sent him to a prestigious international school in Athens. By the age of seventeen, he had become involved with a group of people who belonged to some sort of Satanic cult. At first, their escapades and rituals were interesting and exciting to him, but after a short time, a couple of the older guys in the cult suggested he bring his pretty high school girlfriend into the group.

It was not long before their rituals and demands became more and more intense. The so-called club started controlling his time and, bit by bit, took over his life. He quit school, stopped seeing his old friends, and became a stranger to his family. After about a year or so, he had become consumed by these people and their ideology.

This type of cult was unusual to Greek society, and because of that, the growing organization was very secretive. The thirty or forty members would meticulously plan their meetings far out in the Greek countryside. The big bonfire rallies, dark and sinister costumes, animal sacrifices, and elaborate Satanic rituals completely hypnotized both Yianni and his girlfriend. Part of the brainwashing was that all female members had to have open sex with every male member. Group sex was mandated by the older leaders, which made it sound like they had taken a page out of the 1960's hippy commune booklet that was a part of American culture back then.

Unfortunately, this group of people were not experimenting with sexuality and lifestyle choices; they had evil intentions. In one of their meetings, it was his girlfriend's turn to give herself to all the other men. When Yianni told me a few of the details, I wondered if they had ever been heard in the courtroom.

After he willingly passed his young friend around to the other men, he described a kind of euphoria that gripped the group. In an instant, it was decided that a sacrifice had to be made to Satan. His girlfriend was going to be it.

This friendly young man had somehow gotten caught up in a Charles Manson–type cult and had taken part in the brutal torture and death of his friend. He would spend the rest of his life behind these prison walls. Many months later, he suggested that if I ever got home, I should tell his story to some Hollywood people so they might make a movie about him. He understood that he was exactly where he belonged.

My cell was directly across from Mario and his two Italian pals. Our friendship continued, and every day I was invited to join them for coffee or tea. The two Italians did not speak English, so they were constantly asking Mario to translate. For some reason they were fascinated by me. They were comical little guys, and I liked them.

During the following weeks, I was introduced to an amazing collection of characters. The first man I met who was doing life was Cadillac John, a likable old guy who spent his youth in New York as a gangster. He had been sentenced to life eight years earlier for killing a so-called business partner. I would visit him often to hear his stories and whatever bit of prison wisdom he had for that day. He had completely accepted his fate and adapted himself to getting what little enjoyment he could out of each day. I shuddered to think I might ever end up like him.

One of the saddest stories I heard was that of the Dutchman Gus, a big, tough man in his thirties who was also doing life for smuggling drugs. He had lost his wife, son, and everything he knew of his former life. He had lived in the States for a while and had done some boxing, so he was definitely no one to mess with. He had the biggest hands I had ever seen on a man and was extremely hard knuckled. You could tell that if you ever had to fight him, whether you had a weapon or not, you were going to get hurt. He spoke English well and gravitated to me a few weeks after I got there. I did not mind being seen with him because even the Albanians stayed clear of the Dutchman.

In the beginning, Gus tried to grab onto my energy and my relentless search for the way out of this prison. I would tell him, "Don't ever give up trying to find that door. It will give you purpose and hope. Don't ever accept what they have given you."

I spoke less and less to Gus as the months went by. Thinking of him always made me sad. A strong, young man just beginning his life, he had made an ill-fated decision that shattered every dream he might have had for himself and for the ones he loved. He would spend the next fifty years in this awful place. After a while, he became part of that faceless group of inmates I would see shuffling along, avoiding contact with others and letting himself go to that place where existence is easier because it is without purpose.

Periodically, I noticed a slight unassuming and almost shy man on the fringes of our group. He would make eye contact sometimes, and eventually I waved him over. "Hello, Captain," he said in a heavy accent.

I had been told of him, but this was our first meeting. He was the infamous Russian diamond thief, Andrei. At thirty-five, he was an expert gemologist and knew stones, particularly diamonds. He had worked at the National Museum in Moscow. He was then sent to San Francisco to work with a Russian company, owned by the state, that sold diamonds. He started embezzling and eventually stole millions and millions of dollars' worth of diamonds, selling them on the black market. His lavish lifestyle included mansions, yachts, cars, and everything else that came with sudden wealth and living in America.

It took the Russians two years to figure out what had happened. Andrei did not want to go back to Moscow and figured the Russian agents would find him if he stayed in San Francisco. After hiding his wife and son in Arizona, he took what was left of the diamonds and flew to Brussels to sell them on the black market, eventually getting a few million dollars, which was a fraction of their worth.

He knew he was being tracked by Russian agents but thought he was staying one step ahead of them. When he jumped on the first plane back to New York, via Athens, Greece—big mistake—the Greek authorities arrested him at the airport. Two years later, here he was, the Russians trying desperately to get him back to Moscow and the Greeks refusing extradition.

"You know, Captain," he often exclaimed, "if the Russians get me, I will die in their hands!"

Russian diamond fugitive fights extradition

A JEWELLERY merchant accused of embezzling millions of dollars in gems from a Russian government consortium mounted a final appeal yesterday in Greece's highest court to fight extradition to Russia.

Andrei Kozlenok, 38, is appealing a lower court decision to extradite him after he was arrested on an international warrant at Athens airport in January.

Arguing before the Greek Supreme Court, Kozlenok claimed he could be in danger of being killed if he were returned to Russia. He also claimed Russian officials had harassed both him and his son.

A decision in the case is expected on May 14. If the court rules in favour of extradition, its decision has to be approved by the justice

"A Russian m _____

toring the extradition hearings told reporters afterwards that Kozlenok was simply afraid to face the legitimate charge pending against him:

Eurokinisi

Andrei Kozlenok is led by Greek police to the Supreme Court yesterday in Athens

embezzlement of about $200 million in pre _____ _____

Another suspect in the case, a former Russian interior ministry official, Sergei Dovbysh, was found

dead in February in a courthouse cell in Moscow while awaiting a ___dict in the embezzlement case.

Russian media at the time carried conflicting accounts of Dovbysh's

death, with some saying he died of a heart attack and others saying he was found hanged.

Officials in Russia have accused Kozlenok of fraud in a deal with the Russian State Committee on Metals and Gems while working on behalf of San Francisco-based Golden ADA Inc.

The Russian government filed a lawsuit in San Francisco in 1995, alleging that Golden ADA failed to pay for $165 million in gems and precious metals it received from the Russian consortium.

Officials claim Golden ADA sold the metals and gems without permission and used the money to buy yachts, luxury cars and a mansion.

Russia agreed to a settlement in 1996, subject to approval of the US Internal Revenue Service, which seized Golden ADA's assets last year. The scandal, which some experts say really involved up to $400 million, resulted in the firing of Russia's top diamond official.

(AP)

In a way, I liked and admired this mild-mannered, accountant-type young man. I also loved how he talked incessantly about America. To hear him tell it, every person on Earth should be able to experience America. He spoke as if it were a state of mind, not a country. Andrei had seen his one big chance in life, all be it illegal, and he had taken it. The irony was, with all the millions he had made from the stolen diamonds, at the end of each week, he asked me to buy him cigarettes.

I developed a strict routine and stuck to it. The two hours outside to exercise were critical for me. I would run for an hour, then do full stretch sit-ups on one of the picnic tables, eventually doing two hundred a session. Reverse push-ups were the last thing I did before lockdown. As the days went by, my tension and anxiety grew, and I seemed to need more release through exercise.

There were other inmates who vigorously worked out. I found myself competing, so as to be seen working harder than anyone else out there. Mario and his friends would come over and talk to me while I did my sit-ups, but they were not physical types. Every so often a couple of the guys would get motivated and join me in my routine. None of them lasted too long. In fact, I know they thought I was a little crazy for working so hard.

Lefteri was rarely seen during the day, but on Fridays he would come into the yard. He was superior in martial arts and would stretch and practice his moves. When he invited me to join him in his workouts, I jumped at it, thinking he might teach me a little something. In the beginning, I was slow and awkward, and he would take a little pleasure in hurting me while I learned.

The weeks went by, and I became more competitive. Our sessions started to draw a small crowd. I was certainly no match for Lefteri, but as the combat became more physical, we both found ourselves enjoying Fridays more than any other time. His smile told me in a brotherly way that he liked inflicting pain on me those Fridays, but God, I loved it.

After one of our workouts, Lefteri told me he had my court papers and for me to come down to see him later. I was ecstatic.

It was hard to control my excitement, and the men in my small group were envious of the clout I had with the most powerful inmate in Korydallos.

Lefteri told me it was time to go to work and I should start looking for a lawyer. Little did he know that I had spent a great deal of time talking to anyone who knew anything about Greek lawyers. I had learned who were the best and most powerful in Athens. Who were the cons and who to stay away from. I was determined to learn as much as possible about how this whole system worked.

Lawyers in Greece were first and foremost expert con men. They promised everything, delivered little, and especially with foreign inmates, soaked them for every cent they had. Due to the high profile support I received; I was a very enticing target for these people. This time, I would decide who would represent me.

Two ladies came to see me from the American Embassy. I was the only American in here, and they informed me that high-ranking officials in the embassy were well aware of me and my case. My sister, Doris, they told me, had been the driving force behind an international letter campaign with support coming from my boss, Mr. R., Ross Perot, and several congressmen, particularly Congressman Clay Shaw from my hometown of Fort Lauderdale.

All the people in the yachting community were incredibly supportive. My old friend, John Rule, publisher of the yachting magazine, *The Islander*, in Majorca, Spain, was relentless in his articles informing the international community of my situation. My friends, family, and many others had flooded the desk of the U.S. Ambassador to Greece with letters of support and concern about whether I would receive proper treatment and a fair and speedy court appearance.

The embassy ladies were very thoughtful and brought me some reading material: a 1978 auto mechanics magazine. It was only ten pages, and I think I memorized it in a day. I laughed when they gave it to me, but I knew their intentions were good.

Arrangements were made for Stephanie to fly the ten thousand miles to Athens. She was supposed to meet the two lawyers I had narrowed my choice down to and help me decide on one to represent me. She carried with her several thousand dollars of my money, the up-front retainer. This time, it was going to be my decision, and I had already made up my mind.

That morning, Mario and the boys could tell I was nervous. We stood next to each other, sipping our horrible Greek coffees.

"Why you don't go out in the yard and pick some flowers for her?" he asked, in his broken English.

I looked down at my small friend and testily asked, "What! Are you nuts?"

He looked hurt and said, "You have become an American asshole."

Shocked, I laughed and quickly thought it over. "You're absolutely right," I said.

He continued, "Captain, not every day is a battle."

I said quietly, "Yes, it is, Mario! In a place like this, if you are not prepared to do battle every day, you will lose. Life gives everyone scars, and at the end, you'll know just how well you've done by how few you have and how deep they are."

He turned and walked away.

"Hey, where are you going?" I asked.

He looked back with a smile and said, "I go outside to pick some flowers."

I shook my head as a sad thought about my good Italian friend with the big heart flashed across my mind: he would have trouble surviving his remaining twelve years.

Lefteri met Stephanie outside the visitor area and tried to make her more comfortable, and for this, I was grateful. She was nervous. Once again, another language, another culture for her to navigate through. She sat down across from me. We had not seen each other in five months. My hardness and the mean demeanor I projected left her speechless, unable to mask her look of shock. My physique was tight and gaunt from the rigorous exercise and constant anxiety. I immediately went right to the business at hand, which just happened to be my life.

A look of surprise and hurt came across her face. I did not realize how abrupt and hard my manner was, and later I would regret it. I know the anxious energy I lived with every day must have appeared explosive to her. Nothing else mattered to me except getting out. It frightened her when she realized how different I was from the captain of the *Picante* she used to know.

Stephanie seemed a little listless and lost some of her concentration. I did not know it then, but this ordeal was really taking its toll on her, and she was starting to fade.

Of course, her choice of lawyers was different than mine. She thought I should hire the professor, a soft-spoken man known for his honesty. I tried to explain to her that in this system, I needed someone who, for the most part, lacked principles and understood who to pay and how to do it.

For some reason, people, and particularly Stephanie, thought that when a person was locked in prison, their brain goes dead, and they could no longer think or contribute to the decision-making process. This behavior absolutely drove me insane.

Just as our time ended, she told me Mark S. would be coming to my trial with her. Mark was my boss, Mr. R.'s lawyer and right-hand man. Mr. R. had instructed Mark to attend in order to be my character witness. This news lifted my spirits, something I realized I needed badly.

It seemed Steph and I had no more to say. She took a few steps to leave, looking back with tears, and said softly, "Michael, you have lost your smiling eyes."

I just nodded, saying nothing. She flew home the next day.

12

The prison's population included a variety of nationalities from eastern and western Europe, Africa, and the Far East. Living in close quarters magnified the craziness of people who were mostly bad to begin with. I was the only American, so every once in a while, I would be a target. Besides the occasional extortion attempts, I was also frequently harassed by one particular Greek.

He was an ugly, fat-assed, disgusting man who roamed around with two lackies. Whenever he came near me, he would repeat the only English words he knew: "I like to suck American dick."

At first it made Mario and I burst out laughing, but every time I saw him, he said it. His Peter Lorre like whisper in his thick foreign accent made it sound threatening. I was not afraid of this man and had not responded in any way, but I was getting very tired of constantly watching my back for those assholes.

This day, anger and anxiety, along with the lack of communication with home, had me bouncing off the cellblock walls. I was downstairs in the large area where the showers and toilets were, taking a piss. From behind me, I heard, "I like to suck American dick."

My hair stood on end, and the anger that had consumed me took over. I wanted to put an end to this bullshit right now. I walked up the few steps to the stairwell landing and decided to wait for them—my attitude was that whatever was going to happen was just going to happen.

A few others came up, looked at me, and sensing something was wrong, hurried by. The three Greeks took a couple of steps up before they saw me. I squared off directly with the fat man. Startled, he stopped dead and stared at me. My adrenaline was pumping to the max, and I could almost feel the veins in my neck popping. I felt excitement more than fear, staring straight at the fat Greek.

I said nothing as he gave me a slimy grin but did not repeat his only English words. It seemed like a long time passed. Then he turned around and backed down the steps, disappearing back into the toilets.

I only saw them one more time, and I never heard that English phrase again.

It was well into March and my forty-fifth birthday passed with the thought that I was losing my life, day by day. I had not seen my lawyer since my first talk with him, and I knew that he had received $20,000 of mine from Stephanie. My tension had my metabolism in high gear. I figured he better get his ass over here and sent him a message. He got my message from Lefteri and came to see me with the news that my trial date had been set April 28th.

It astounded my pals in prison that I had gotten a date in under a year. I knew it usually took much longer, so I figured the media and all the pressure from everyone involved had helped. I found out later that the money my lawyer paid to certain people helped more.

On one particular day, I was standing with Mario and friends on the main corridor where we drank coffee and shared prison gossip. We were watching the usual crazy, constant motion of men scheming, gangs in groups eyeing the others, constant harassment, and the never-ending cacophony that goes with four hundred men talking and shouting at once, all melting together and becoming a very loud hum.

In the prison environment, the mental endurance of some is less than others. It is well documented what happens to individuals who cannot endure the physical and mental anguish that comes with the complete loss of hope and knowing their remaining years will be spent in confinement.

On this morning in cellblock B, another man had gone to that place. My head was turned, listening to Mario, when suddenly, the constant prison hum ceased and a painful scream echoed, followed by the most incredible sound I've ever heard when this man landed head-first on the concrete corridor. He had dived off the third floor without any warning, and the sound of his head hitting cement cannot be described. It was like no other sound or noise I have ever heard before or since. It stayed with me, and when I think of that tragedy, I hear that noise precisely. It was like a huge rock inside a pumpkin being dropped from the third floor. It was a hard, solid SPLAT! combined with somewhat of a ripping and cracking, and that still does not explain it.

But we all knew it for what it was the moment it occurred. It had a sickening finality to it. Quickly turning, I saw the body about fifty feet from me and was struck by the huge amount of blood. It literally looked like a small lake surrounding a lifeless mass of flesh. For some reason, I wondered how much blood the human body held. Thinking this when all hell broke loose, watching the chaos with calmness, I knew I was becoming seriously calloused and losing a part of me that was being replaced by something else I did not like.

The nervous, frightened feeling I lived with every day had me in constant motion, from the minute the cell doors opened in the morning until lockdown at night. The stress had started to take a toll. I was having chest pains and trouble breathing at times. I became afraid of becoming ill or having a heart attack, knowing I would probably die before I received medical attention.

I was told it took weeks to get in to see the prison doctor, so I decided to mention my problem to Lefteri. I had made up my mind not to ask him any favors unless it was especially important, but I had to get help soon. I was surprised when, the very next day, he came to get me, and I was escorted out the cellblock gates. Lefteri himself, along with a prison guard, guided me across the compound to a long, narrow building, which served as the prison hospital. We entered at one end of the building and stood in front of a single desk.

Behind this check-in area, I could see down a single long hallway that had rooms on each side. The place was full of prison personnel and inmates. It seemed to me that everywhere I went, the loud, chaotic, atmosphere followed, and their so-called hospital was no exception.

After a few minutes, we walked through and started down the long corridor. The walls were a dirty yellow color, with several areas of paint starting to peel off. It seemed like Lefteri knew everyone. People came up and greeted him with smiles and a few words as we made our way down the hall. We reached the last room at the end, and he told me to sit down in the single chair facing the open door. He had his back turned to me, but I could see him talking with one of the people inside. When he came out, he told me he had explained my problem to the doctor and would be back in a while.

I sat there mesmerized, watching the scene taking place inside the open room. The doctor caught my attention because of the dirty, blood-stained white coat he had on over his grubby street clothes. But even more compelling was the cigarette he had hanging from the corner of his mouth. It jerked up and down as he spoke, and I caught myself leaning forward on the edge of my chair, staring at the inch-long ashes, anticipating their fall. It seemed everyone smoked in this part of the world, and some had developed a talent for being able to talk and even eat while smoking their dangling cigarettes.

This doctor was so good at it, I thought it was glued on. He was trying to take blood from an inmate seated on the only chair inside the stark room. There was not any real medical equipment, but he did have the help of a woman I guessed was his nurse. They were having difficulty drawing the man's blood. After a couple of unsuccessful tries, with blood spurting everywhere, the three of them erupted into an enormous shouting match.

As I watched this act play out over the next half hour, I could not help but think how typical it was of the entire place. I caught myself imagining what a hilarious comedy skit this would have made for *Saturday Night Live*. Here it was again, one of those scenes that was so absurd I caught myself laughing as I sat alone in the middle of all these people in this crazy foreign place. Finally, the comedy played itself out, and it was my turn. No way was I going to let them try and take my blood.

The doctor shouted a couple of things at me in Greek, scribbled something on a piece of paper, and that was it. What the hell was that, I wondered. As it turned out, Lefteri took the note and came back with an inhaler that helped my breathing a great deal.

That night, back in lockdown, I told Mario and our group about my entertaining day. We all had a good laugh, and Mario reminded me I would not have had such a good day if it hadn't been for Lefteri. But by this time, he knew better than to ask me for an introduction.

13

As my court date approached, I was fanatic about preparing and learning what was in the Greek court documents from so long ago. Lefteri translated just about every word and was amazed at how obviously corrupt and deceptive my arrest warrant was. He said that even for the Greek system, this was very blatant; they had made no effort to cover themselves or their payoffs.

A few days later, I sat across from Lefteri in his cell. He was halfway through the thick binder of documents when he slowly looked up at me. With a curious look on his face and shaking his head, he said, "Michael, this paper right here is the port customs debarkation paper with your signature on the date you left with the boat. Signed by customs agents and stamped with approval." He continued, "This is absolute proof that you have had a portion of your life stolen from you. You do not deserve to be here."

I managed a half-laugh, mixed with sadness. "So now you believe me?"

"According to everyone here, this prison should be empty," he responded sarcastically. As he read the Greek documents, Lefteri learned the details of the corrupt footsteps the Greek yacht owner had taken when he initiated the warrant for my arrest. I told him that an investigation of the man's background had uncovered a history of fraud. It had become clear to my family and myself that the motive behind his reporting the boat stolen must have been an illegal insurance scam. Unfortunately, it had been at my expense.

Every day became a drain on my nerves. It was a constant struggle getting through each long hour without making a mistake that could get me hurt or killed, or worse, in trouble that would lead to more time. Added to that was the difficulty of communicating with the people who held my future in their hands.

The court date was just ten days away, and I had not talked with my lawyer for two weeks. I wanted to be assured that the money had been paid to the proper people. I did not want to take any chances, although I knew they would find me guilty of something because I was a foreigner. If it were a minimal charge, I hoped I would be released (providing all monetary commitments by my attorney had been met).

Finally, my attorney came to see me six days before my court date with all the answers to my agonizing questions. He informed me that the panel of five judges had just been selected yesterday. I understood he could not tell me how he would handle paying these people.

He did appear confident, and his body language said, "Don't worry," as did his words. Then, in the next breath, he mentioned how impressive the material and character reference my sister, Doris, Stephanie, and so many others had worked so incredibly hard to put together on my behalf. He paused before delivering the bombshell: "I'm sorry, Michael, but the evidence in the Greek court papers and the work your family has done will not be used or even seen by the judges in the first trial."

My voice was loud and angry, rumbling down the visitor's hallway. Every man turned my way as I made it clear, noticeably clear, that there would only be one trial. "I've given you the money and it's your responsibility to make sure this is it," I said. I was not trying to sound threatening, but the sudden silence in the visitor's room, and the startled look on his face, left no doubt...that's exactly how I sounded.

It finally arrived: my day in court. I would have my chance to face that despicable person and the evil, labyrinthine system that had purposely stolen the most precious of all things in life: time. The psychological endurance test I had gone through the past year had taken its pound of flesh. I knew I was nearly beaten. The fatigue I felt cut right to the bone. My physical and mental aging processes had fast forwarded. I had to get off this emotional roller coaster, and I had to get off now! I needed to go home. I needed the security and peace that would allow me to rest.

Giant butterflies filled my stomach as I was led into the court-room. It was pandemonium. The room opened up into adjacent areas, where other trials were taking place. Greek courts do not resemble any legal proceedings we are used to. It is a circus, complete with the judges as clowns. All these Greeks trying to out-shout each other, each one thinking what he had to say was of critical importance.

My position, once again, was behind the podium in the middle of all this chaos. There were Steph and Mark; they quickly came over and greeted me. It made me feel so much better having them there. The American Embassy ladies were in the back, and the lawyers stood on both sides of me.

Of course, the five judges were seated up high, looking down on me. It struck me how they dressed. No black robes, just street clothes, with all of them wearing short-sleeved, striped shirts that had a little cuff on the sleeve. Actually, they looked a bit shabby. The shouting in Greek continued, and it seemed that my case was being interrupted by people involved in other cases. A lady came and stood next to me; she was the translator. This circus carried on for another fifteen minutes. Then the chief judge looked down and asked the lady to speak to me. They wanted to know if I had anything to say.

I spoke loudly and was profoundly serious as I looked up at each one. I wanted to make them understand that a year of my life had been taken from me for something I did not do. In the mid-dle of this circus, I felt it was impossible to convey what had happened to me. Noticing a quizzical look crossing the judge's face, I stopped. I realized my translator was not doing such a good job.

The five of them left the courtroom for their decision. I remained standing there with a guard next to me. My lawyer stood off to my left and said almost nothing during this calamity. He came closer and let me know that he thought everything would be okay. I wanted to believe him so bad, but I detected a slight lack of confidence. Mark and Stephanie were able to talk to me. Mark could not believe what was taking place. He would not have believed this was a legal proceeding if he had not witnessed the fiasco himself.

The five men quietly reappeared. There was no protocol, no bailiff saying, "All rise for the judges." The chief judge started speaking, and for the first time that day, the room grew quiet. There must have been eighty to one hundred people going in and out of the room. My interpreter smiled and whispered to me, "The first major theft charge is dismissed."

A kind of light began to creep into my heart.

"The second major theft charge," she continued, "is dismissed by the court."

Continuing in Greek, the sound of which was harsh and unpleasant to my ears, the judges dismissed all major theft charges. My lawyer was grinning. I glanced back at Steph and Mark, and I could see someone was translating for them; they both had big smiles. For that brief moment, right then, I could picture myself being home.

The chief judge kept on talking/shouting as the Greeks do. Interested others in the court started shouting their conversations as well. The judges were finished talking and were getting up, moving away from that high, long, condescending position that people with any degree of power in this part of the world always seemed to need.

My long-anticipated day in court was clearly over, having lasted about a half an hour. The front area of the court filled with people. Glancing around, I anxiously tried to find my lawyer in the crowd. The translator next to me spoke sharply in my ear. "Guilty of misdemeanor mischief," she said. No one ever explained what that was, and we later learned that it was also never explained in their so-called court documents.

She just stared at me without emotion, "You are sentenced to three years."

It was pure reflex; my head snapped toward the five scruffy judges. Unable to control myself, I released a piercing scream, "NOOOOO!" The sound echoed off the ceiling, carrying my shock and disbelief and rising above the other shouting in the room.

For a moment, everyone stopped and stared. I saw nothing. Immediately, the guards were at my sides, moving me toward the downstairs holding cell. Panic mixed with frustration made my head feel like it weighed eighty pounds, like I was falling and could not stop.

I tried to find Stephanie and Mark in the chaos, but nothing seemed vivid to me. It felt like I had suffered a concussion. My body was so heavy, I could not hold my head up. My eyes would not focus. From behind, arms wrapped around me, and both Mark and Stephanie were holding me.

Mark kept saying, "Stay strong, stay strong, we will get you home."

I wanted to thank him for coming, but I could not get it out. Steph and I just looked at each other. How many times had those eyes cried for me this past year? I should have been going home with her today. That is what we had planned.

She said she would come to see me tomorrow before they went home. I just shook my head, unable to speak.

Parting the crowd, the guards firmly guided me downstairs to the holding cell. I stopped, turned around, and finally managed a harsh whisper. "Don't come to see me," I said. Struggling to hold back overwhelming emotions, my voice cracked. "Thank you for everything you've done for me."

Downstairs in the holding cell, I lay down on the floor feeling bloodless, completely drained of light, of hope, of life. Lying there with my eyes closed, I could not think of anything except the numb feeling of knowing I would be back in lockdown tonight. I opened my eyes when I heard my lawyer calling from outside the cell gate.

Leaning against the bars, I tried to listen to what he said. He told me it had been too crowded to speak to me in court. He wanted to say congratulations but thought better after seeing my reaction. He tried to explain the situation, telling me I would only do ten months because of time already served. My time in Turkish prisons counted double in the Greek system. I just lowered my head, still saying nothing.

"In the Greek courts, as a foreigner, you won! You can appeal this decision, but it will take about eighteen months to get a court date. Also, the court has the option of reversing this decision and giving you a longer sentence."

The words went on but seemed more and more meaningless. "You must understand," he continued, "this was a big victory for you. The charges were severe, and this is not like America. Here, you must be found guilty of something. They dismissed everything. Just a misdemeanor. I know you think this sentence is big, but in this country, it is not."

I raised my head and in my raspy voice said, "I cannot stay in this place another year!" I knew he could feel the burn in my eyes. I sounded desperate and made no effort to disguise the threatening tone in my voice. "Find me a way out of here. It doesn't matter what it takes or how it's done; just get me out." I meant what I had said more than anything I had ever said in my life.

He understood, looked away and said, "I'll come and see you next week. We might have one more option."

14

I did not leave my cell for nearly a week. Mario and a few others came by to offer congratulations. They all thought the same thing: I had beaten the Greek system. To them, ten months was nothing.

Serious depression set in. I had no energy for conversation or for anything else. I just wanted to sleep, wake up, and have it be time to go home.

After many days of this, Lefteri finally stopped at my cell. He knew I had crashed and burned emotionally, but he was not going to allow that to continue. I was alone in my cell when he came in. The first thing he demanded was that I take down the makeshift curtain I had rigged for privacy. "That's dangerous in here," he said. "You can't see who's coming at you."

I guess he felt it was time to pass on some wisdom in the way only he was able.

"I was in the U.S. Army, stationed mostly down in Texas," Lefteri continued. "I am a Greek and an American, and I was extremely fortunate to be given the absolute best training, education, and discipline in the world. After I served my time, I came back here, started a family, and went to work in top security for one of our most powerful politicians. During the elections, several years ago, my party lost, and Greek politics being what they are, I made some enemies. I was set up and arrested with a few weapons in one of our vehicles. They charged me with smuggling arms. I was given a life sentence. It took five years for my appeal, during which time I decided to learn the system and fight. I represented myself, and my sentence was reduced to eight years. I only have a few more left. Like you, I won. What I am saying, Michael, is never give up. There might be other ways out of here, but if you quit, you will do the time they gave you. By the way, ten months is like a weekend by Greek standards."

Turning, he told me I would see him Friday for our exercise routine, and then he abruptly left. It sunk in a few minutes later that he expected me to be out there. He made it sound like I would let him down if I were not.

It was difficult to shed the deep depression I had fallen into. All I wanted to do was sleep. At the end of that week, another man stopped by my cell very unexpectedly. I did not know this guy, but he knew who I was. He told me he had observed me for a couple of months and heard I had found my way out. He was an older man of about sixty-five from Finland with a slender build, small features, and bright blue eyes that projected nothing but honesty. He was very soft-spoken and seemed like a genuinely nice person. I could hear the sadness in his voice as he continued his story. He and his wife had come to Athens, Greece, as tourists. They had saved some of their pension money to travel and were extremely interested in the history and ruins Greece had to offer.

On their fourth day visiting Athens, they had already toured the famous Acropolis, Parthenon, and many of the other magnificent ancient structures, so they decided to spend this day, a warm one, walking the back streets and neighborhoods of the old city, which is full of interesting sights. They passed by an old house, small and unassuming, but with a nice orange tree in the garden. Not thinking it would be of any consequence, they picked two oranges. At that precise moment, an old Greek woman came out of the house yelling and screaming, waving her arms as if the sky were falling. The two old Finnish tourists, startled by the Greek woman's theatrics, scampered down the street. A few blocks away, police pulled up and stopped, questioned them, and abruptly arrested them both. The Greek woman pressed charges, and the next thing the old couple knew, they were imprisoned in Korydallos.

She was put in the woman's section, and he was sent to cell-block B. Here this man was, fourteen months later, confused and completely distraught. He had just gotten the tragic and terribly stressful news that his wife had been beaten very badly by the Albanian women and taken to the prison hospital. The pain on this man's gentle face knocked me over. I wondered how it could be possible that this elderly man would spend this much time in prison for stealing *two fucking oranges*!

Listening to this poor man's story and imagining something like that happening to my own mother, I could feel the seething anger I had been living with for so long start to surface again. Anger had embedded itself deep inside me, and at that time, I didn't real-ize the internal fight I would have in the years to come trying to get rid of it, or the anguish I would suffer as a consequence.

He said he came to talk with me because he hoped I might be able to offer some knowledge or suggest some way that would jump-start his efforts to speed up this awful process. He told me others had said I must have connections because of my movements, the men I associated with in Korydallos, and most of all, because I had been able to get myself a quick court date.

I could not tell him any great secret to find his way out of this labyrinth, but the anger I felt at hearing his story energized me, raising a second wind of passion bent on getting myself out of this hellhole sooner than anyone might think. During the previ-ous months, I had avoided being a conduit for any of my group to Lefteri. But I thought this Finnish man would be someone he would want to meet.

I returned to the yard with a vengeance, feeling the eyes fol-lowing me as I came out. Mario and his friends were stationed in their usual place with big smiles on their faces as I approached to say hello. My exercise routine became more intense as I tried to release the anger inside. I wanted it noticed how fanatic I was with the pace I set in the exercise yard.

Two weeks had passed since my trial, and it was well into May. The tension around me was thick. I could not bring myself to face another year inside this place. I hated everything Greek, and I started to verbalize it.

One morning, I kept hearing some sort of announcement over the cellblock loudspeaker. I could not follow what it was saying, so I went over to ask Mario.

"They want volunteers to clean out the boiler room," he said. "Downstairs."

I thought about it. The boilers were one level below the showers, it was the source of the hideous smell that sickened you when using the toilets or showers. The room was always locked, and, through the years, prison cats had made the place a burial ground.

Of course, not a single Greek out of the few hundred in the yard stepped forward. Something grabbed me, a screw-everything-Greek attitude! Abruptly, I said to Mario, "Follow me," and headed for the cellblock gate. I needed him to translate for me.

I told him to tell the guards I would be their volunteer to clean the boiler room. He looked at me with a half-smile and just shook his head. I exclaimed, "All Greeks are loudmouth pussies." In Greek, it sounded something like *pousty malakas*. No way was Mario going to repeat that to the guards.

Word got out, and later that evening a few people dropped by to offer advice. Cadillac John stopped by to tell me with a grin that they ask every year for volunteers to clean the boiler room. He had been in prison eight years and nobody had ever volunteered until now. He just shook his head and left. A few others came by to find out if it was really true.

The next day, followed down the cellblock corridor by Mario and the Italians singing the *Rocky* theme. I was escorted downstairs with a shovel, gloves, and some plastic bags. I fixed a plastic bag like a poncho, putting this on with a rag tied around my nose and mouth. I had to psyche myself up; the smell was horrendous when the guard opened the door.

A crowd gathered up the three-story stairwell. I am sure they thought the American was either stupid, crazy, or both. I gagged when I entered the dark room full of skeletons and carcasses that must have been there for years. It took me a couple of hours, hauling out bags of rotten cats. I worked with a frenzy. With sweat pouring off me, I finished and climbed back up the stairwell. Mario and friends were in the front of the large group that had gathered to watch the spectacle. They cheered in their funny way, handed me water, and patted me on the back. I spotted Lefteri off in the crowd with a big smile on his face.

I just shrugged toward him and headed back to my cell. I knew the reason I had done the cat clean-out was a reaction to being pissed off at the Greeks and everything Greek. But they just saw a crazy American captain, rather than my contempt for their culture. From that time on, I received small acknowledgments from inmates and a little recognition from the guards whenever I came close to the gates. They also gave me free ice cream, which I was able to pass out to a few of the guys in my group on Wednesday nights. It became a regular event my small group looked forward to.

We even moved our social meeting spot from Mario's cell closer to the cellblock gates where the ice cream was passed out. Everyone loved Wednesday nights after that, stopping by to chat and hoping to receive a free ice cream. It became the highlight of our weeks, and when the ice cream did not show one Wednesday, we were all devastated. Another week went by before I could hand out my free ice creams to the Italians and some others. Such a silly and simple thing to look forward to, but it generated good feelings and a few laughs. It made cleaning out the dead cats worth it.

The thought of having to live in this awful place for another year was like an explosion inside me, leaving me feeling more alone than ever. After my trial, I felt like the people at home had resigned themselves to the fact that I was going to be here a while and had just given up.

It became more difficult to reach Stephanie by phone. Something was different. Even across the ten thousand miles, I could hear a distinct difference in her choice of words and tone of speech. I knew it had been a long, lonely struggle for her, and I worried she would not be there at the end. When I was able to communicate with her, I know I was sharp and demanding. I could not stand to hear comments like, "I pray for you," or, "This will make you stronger." I was already strong enough. I did not need this experience to make me stronger.

I knew I could not survive another year in here. But Stephanie and the others at home had no idea what it was really like inside a place like this. It was not their fault; it's impossible to fully comprehend what it's like unless you have lived it. The pressure of existing in a place where life and death is all around you every minute of every day takes a huge toll both physically and mentally.

There was no way I could explain it; I did not even try. I was obsessed with getting out of this place, and I would not waste valuable energy on anything else.

The daily fight against the stress and panic had me wound tight. I am sure I appeared to be bouncing off the walls. Mario and others tried to warn me, thinking I might get myself hurt or in trouble. The biggest hurdle I had in my fight to get out was the horrible difficulty in using the phones. When I noticed that the guys who had the job of cleaning the cellblock every night after lockdown had free and uncrowded access to the few pay phones, I made it my mission to find out how I could get one of these prized jobs.

I soon learned that, like everything else in Korydallos, corruption dictated that it came with a price. The American captain's price was going to be the outrageous amount of twelve thousand dollars. I was so desperate to have the access to the phones without the vicious Albanians breathing down my neck that I set about trying to make this happen. After about two weeks of pushing people hard and relentlessly trying to find a way to make this work, I was rattled by some serious news Lefteri passed on to me: a message had been dispatched through the prison grapevine that if the American captain was able to get a job on the cleaning detail, it wouldn't be for long. I would be hurt! It took guys years in here to get a job like that, there was no way I would be allowed to leapfrog my way to the front of the line.

15

It was the end of May: warm weather and the start of another summer. It was a very depressing time as I realized it had been almost a year since all this had started. Something was strange about this hot May morning. Making my way upstairs, I noticed how quiet it was and how very few inmates were outside their cells. The yard was not open yet, so everybody was still inside. I knew Lefteri was working in the canteen room on the second floor. He would know what was happening. I never got used to the language thing. God, it pissed me off not really knowing the things going on around me.

Suddenly, the prison sirens started blaring. I could hear them going off all over the compound. Chaos erupted in an instant, starting at the far end of the cellblock. A minute before, it had been calm; now the noise escalated as group after group of inmates quickly banded together from the third floor down. I could see it all developing from where I was watching at the other end of the second floor.

My hair stood on end; adrenaline poured into my blood and fear and panic filled me. The Albanians! They were throwing steel cots over the balconies, along with mattresses, chairs, tables, and absolutely anything they could get their hands on. It was a riot!

Looking at the garbage raining down and the inmates running for their cells, I saw Mario just outside his door frantically trying to get my attention. I could not hear him, but he was pointing at my cell, telling me to get down there and get inside. He made it clear that I had better do it right now! He dashed inside and shut his cell door.

The riot was turning violent. Like a wave of insanity out of control, it was rolling right toward me. Twenty, maybe thirty Albanians were using chair legs for clubs and any other weapons they could find as they picked out cells to ransack. They blocked the way back to my cell, beating anyone in their way. I knew they would like to catch the American captain just to make a point.

I had to find a place to hide NOW! The noise was deafening, with the sirens, the screaming and shouting, and heavy objects hitting the ground floor. A few fires had been set as well, making it all very confusing. I was in the middle of a war zone! I crouched and backed up against the back wall, trying to figure something out and hoping to become invisible.

I could hear someone shouting my name directly across from me. Lefteri was peering out the canteen door about fifty feet away, yelling at me to get my ass over there. I had about a minute before they would be on me. I sprinted and ducked inside as Lefteri locked the door behind me.

Of course, he would have the key to the canteen. Inside the room with him was Yianni, my Satanic killer friend. This was a sanctuary because it was not safe in your cell; you could not lock your doors. Lefteri explained that he had only found out about this plan a little while ago. It had been organized by the Albanian leaders in the other cellblocks. They were rioting to protest the crackdown on their drug business. "This is the best place to be," he said. "If you get caught outside, you'll be hurt by the Albanians or the Greek riot squad."

We climbed up on a ledge to look out the barred window. From where we stood, we could see dozens of military types dressed in riot gear: face masks, shields, clubs, etc. The worst of the uprising was taking place in cellblock C. After several minutes, tear gas was shot into the blocks. With brutal force and no regard for who was who, the chaos quickly ended.

The riot squad came fast and hard into cellblock B, but the Albanians had already quieted down somewhat. We hid inside the locked canteen, hearing the heavy boots of the riot police and the loud squawk of the bullhorn. Lefteri said, "They are telling all inmates to get to their cells. Put your hands on your head, Michael, and keep moving." There were three others with us when he opened the canteen door. Four or five of the riot squad spotted us right away.

They ran at us with full body armor, swinging their thick, black batons and looking seriously dangerous. I was violently pushed toward the stairs by Lefteri. He tried to say something to me as he looked back and scrambled down the stairwell.

Suddenly, I was hit with such force on the back of my thighs, it buckled my knees, and I fell to all fours. The pain was so excruciating that it literally knocked the wind out of me. I fought for breath, getting to my feet and sprinting down the stairs and across to my cell. I fell inside the door, face down onto my bunk.

My head was spinning; the throbbing ache pounded with every beat of my heart. I could not move. I had never felt such agonizing pain. I stood and asked the Jap to help me take off my jeans. He just whistled when he saw the back of my right thigh. The bruise was about six inches in diameter. The blood had already turned black, not blue. It stood off my leg a good half inch. I had never seen a bruise like it. That's what Lefteri had been trying to tell me: "Haul ass! Don't get caught at the back!" I had that bruise a long, long time.

The Albanians had been inside Mario's cell and ransacked the Italian's belongings. The worst that happened was one of our little Italian friends had his long beard cut off with a makeshift razor by a couple of the marauders. They skipped my cell, but that night the riot squads came back and stripped every single cell in the block.

After clean-up, we were locked in our cells for five days straight. The other cellblocks were not allowed out for two weeks.

I was pushing my lawyer hard to come and talk to me. I wanted to know what he thought might be my chance of early release. His

117

attitude seemed to be that it was all over for me, and I was lucky to only have another year to serve. I was going to straighten him out on that.

He finally showed up and explained that there was a hearing in a few weeks that would allow foreigners to ask for release pending their appeal court dates. He also said he had never seen a foreigner released at this kind of hearing and that applying for an appeal was a gamble. The judges could change my sentence to a longer one. If I wanted to take the risk, I would need a Greek sponsor with an address, and I would be required to check into the local police station every few days.

My excitement was hard to conceal. We both knew none of these conditions would be serious obstacles. My lawyer tried to downplay the chances of me getting out, but in my overwhelming optimism, I sensed that he was genuinely enthusiastic. I suddenly stopped in mid-sentence and looked directly into his eyes. "What's the bottom line?" I asked. "Seven thousand dollars," he replied. I nodded. After all, I was used to the system by now. "But this time," he added, "you don't have to pay until after we hear the judge's decision."

That was good news to me, and I was excited to call home. After a tortuous and always dangerous wait for the phones, I picked up the receiver, willing Stephanie to be there.

"Hello?" Her voice was distant and far away. "Steph! Listen. I need seven thousand for an appeal." For a few seconds she said nothing. "Michael?" "What's wrong?" I was suddenly anxious and agitated. She did not sound like she cared.

In the next moment, the dark and isolated world I lived in became even darker. Over the loud and relentless hum of the cellblock behind me, I heard her say softly, "I'm seeing another man."

I did not respond. I could not. She kept repeating my name from halfway around the world, but that awful panicky feeling came over me, giving me a gut-wrenching ache that hurt as bad as anything a man can feel.

I think I slammed the receiver down. I do not remember. Feeling numb and out of breath, I fought my way out of the crowd around the phones. I stayed in my cell the next couple of days, trying to think everything through. I was devastated, betrayed by the one person I needed to be there for me to survive.

Cadillac John came by to visit. This was unusual for him, as he rarely deviated from his routine. He had heard through the cellblock grapevine the news of Stephanie and her new boyfriend. The only person I had told was Mario, but it did not bother me that he'd shared the news with anyone else, especially Cadillac John.

"Don't be judgmental," he tried to tell me. "You're living in a far more serious place. You have to rise above the things you can't control and keep focused on your own objectives." I just gave him a blank stare.

"You got to forgive her. After all, she's been through hell because of what happened to you." He ended his words of wisdom by telling me that the unwritten prison handbook says girlfriends are usually faithful for about a year and married women for a year and a half.

I didn't feel any better after his pep talk, but it did put a small smile on my face, thinking that here I was in a foreign prison, ten thousand miles from home, taking advice from an old man doing life for murder.

The hearing was in two weeks, on June 24th. I finally called home again and reached Stephanie, who was frantic at not hearing from me. She begged me not to cut off communication. I tried to tell her I understood and not to worry about all that other stuff. I was nice on the phone and explained about the court hearing coming up. "All that matters is to get home," I said. "Everything will work out after that."

I told her I needed the seven thousand dollars to be paid only after the judge's decision. She did not answer, and my time ran out, so I was not able to get as much information as I wanted. "I'll call again tomorrow!" I exclaimed.

During the next several days, I was not able to reach Stephanie. The phones were so difficult to use. The waiting and the daily trouble surrounding them made it incredibly frustrating. Less than a week before the hearing, I was lying in my bunk late in the evening after lockdown. My cellmate, the small Japanese man who had killed his shipmate, was pacing in our cell and ranting on about some stupid-ass thing having to do with soccer's World Cup. I was not listening, but finally he insisted I answer his question.

I sat up and noticed the look on his face. He had worked himself into a frenzy. His eyes were bulging and sweat poured off him as he started to scream at me. Suddenly, my hair stood on end. Realizing this was not an ordinary situation, I stood up and tried to calm whacko Japo down. He screamed at the top of his lungs, wanting to know what the World Cup trophy was made of.

He started to throw things. Quickly, I tried to figure what he wanted to hear that would appease him. "I'm not sure, buddy, but I think it's made of gold."

An inmate's worst nightmare was about to happen: a fight with your cellmate after lockdown. There was not anything I could do but face it. The Jap was only about five-foot-nothing but was on the wacky side and had already proved himself a killer. Just as I stepped back, he leaped at me with fists flying. The sounds he made were frightening, making me think I was fighting some hari-kari nutcase. Fortunately, he had no weapons but landed a few punches to my face and head. It felt like I was trying to get the little monster Chuckie off me. My fury was immediate. I managed to hold him at arm's length and landed a crunching fist to his cheek.

He staggered back, and I ripped a mattress off the bunk and threw it at him. The cell was being torn apart. I went after him in a brutal rage, hard and fast. It was either him or me. All my pent-up rage and hostility exploded, and I got him in a headlock using all my strength.

He could not move or breathe. My forearms and biceps were ripping. I had him in a death grip. "You're dead, motherfucker!" I screamed.

He stopped struggling, and I came to my senses, sweat streaming from every pore as I slowly let him loose.

Humbled and quiet, he climbed up to his bunk without saying a word. It was over as quickly as it had started. Needless to say, I had no sleep that night. The next day, I got myself moved to a cell across the corridor and near Mario.

The day of the court hearing arrived—my last shot at getting out. The courtroom was full of foreigners all asking for early release. My lawyer was in the room, but I did not get a chance to speak to him. I was seated in the back with about thirty others. Only one judge presided this time. He started to read through the applications, and one after another, they were denied.

That all-too-familiar feeling of disappointment settled over me. He had gone through almost everyone. I was just about the last one, and all of them had been denied with a loud "Óxee," which is Greek for "No."

I heard my name called and stood up as required. The judge read a few sentences in Greek, and with a bang of his gavel, he said, "Nai!" (Greek for yes)

I was stunned, not sure if I had been granted release or not. I looked for my lawyer, catching his big smiling face and his thumbs-up.

I needed to get the seven thousand dollars to my lawyer right away now that I had been granted release. I finally got a hold of Stephanie and explained the outcome of the proceeding. She did not believe me and kept repeating the same words, "We don't have much money left, Michael." She was afraid I was being conned.

"I'm not being conned!" I said. "I'm telling you; I was in the courtroom. It is already done! I just have to pay."

My time ended at the phone again, her last words resounding in my mind. "I don't want to send the money," she had said. "Don't want to send the money...don't want to send the money..."

I was livid. It was practically impossible to talk on the phone under these conditions. I would call again tomorrow thinking I would make her understand. The sooner she got it here, the sooner I would get out.

Frantic was an understatement for how I felt. Any kind of sleep or normal routine was out of the question. As soon as the cells were opened in the morning, I dashed for the phone lines. Already, dozens of guys were lined up. It was one of my last chances to reach Steph and get my money sent. It was the first of July, and I knew if she did not do it right away, it would go into the Fourth of July holiday weekend in the States. I wanted so badly to be home for the Fourth, always my favorite holiday. It ate me up inside.

As I waited in the always-tense phone lines, my thoughts were chaotic. I was now twenty-nine days shy of one year of being locked inside these despicable foreign prisons for something I had not done. The stress and tension of not completely understanding the things happening around me had taken its toll. I could not go through another day of the constant fighting and trying to figure out what people were saying. Not speaking the language compounded my difficulties in lockdown.

Knowing the pace at which civil affairs, or anything for that matter, moved in Greece had me very worried. I can only explain it by saying that the Spanish word "Mañana" (tomorrow) has a sense of urgency for the Greeks. Greek government workers start closing down at the end of July and are gone the entire month of August.

I could not fathom Stephanie not believing I had been granted early release, and I had two minutes to make her understand from ten thousand miles away. I was on edge.

I heard her say hello and I spoke quickly in a kind, firm voice. "Steph, I can be out of here in a matter of hours. Just send my money to the lawyer."

"You don't understand," she said. "That will leave me with only $5,000. You just do not understand what kind of stress I am dealing with here. I need that money!"

I gripped the phone so tightly with both hands, I thought I would crush it. Where did Stephanie go? This was not Stephanie on the line. This did not sound like the Stephanie who had been my partner in life these past years. This person had no frigging clue what real stress was. In a helpless panic, I snapped.

Not hearing or seeing anything behind me, I cupped the receiver and replied in a deep, vicious tone that even startled me. "You had better send my money, and you had better do it today!" My words and tone pierced those ten thousand miles of wire like she was next to me. I could almost see her step back from her phone. She started to cry, and I knew I was going home.

I held the receiver with both hands tightly to my mouth and ear, my head down, my body tense. I could feel the gang and hear the shouting building behind me in that hideous Greek language. But there was no way I was giving up this phone until I heard her agree.

I do not remember if I actually heard the explosion of the pay phone being hit and shattering in pieces and falling off the wall in front of me. Still holding the receiver, I turned, and towering over me was the biggest man in the cellblock. Six-foot-five with huge bodybuilder arms and an immense chest, he was an enforcer doing life. The Greeks respectfully called him The Manga. I could not see or hear anything beyond my boiling anger. I stuck the receiver of the phone inches from his ugly face, my neck veins bulging and eyeballs popping out. I screamed at the top of my lungs that I was going to stick this up his ass so far that he would be speaking with it at the other end.

He understood nothing I said, but he could see that I had gone over the edge, that I had lost it. This Manga could hurt or even kill me, but he just looked down at me, shrugged, and pushed his way back through the crowd. My anger had taken me to that extremely dangerous place in my head where I was not afraid to be hurt. Perhaps he had seen it in my eyes.

The next thing I remember was Lefteri sitting next to me on my bunk, telling me if I did not calm down, I would not have to worry about getting home. "Lay low," he said. "Hang around in the cell for a couple days." So, I did.

A few days later, I was summoned to the visitor's room. I thought it was probably my lawyer wondering where the money was.

Sure enough, I spotted him right away standing down at the end with a giant smile on his face. My heart leapt, and I practically ran toward him. I suddenly realized I sort of liked my lawyer. Mr. Tzakis Kehoglou was a bit of a shyster, but a good, kind man. He just liked money, especially dollars.

"Did she send the money?" I asked.

"Yes, you will be getting out soon. Probably in a couple of weeks."

I instantly bristled. "No, no, no. You mean a couple of days, don't you? If I am still here in August, you know nothing will happen until September." I looked directly at him, quietly asking to please get me out of here soon. The look on his face told me he understood the seriousness of what I had asked.

He truly looked concerned. "Are you all right, Michael?" he asked.

"Mr. Kehoglou, I have to get out of here now! I'm not sure I can survive much longer," I pleaded.

"Michael, I like you a lot," he replied. "You have been through so much and have been an extraordinarily strong man. I will do all I can to make this happen sooner."

I grabbed his hand to shake, my grip perhaps a little too strong. I did not say another word, but he knew. I started back toward my cell, and then turned to find him still staring at me. "Thanks for everything you have done for me," I said.

He just gave me a big smile. I liked that.

Walking back to cellblock B, I knew I had given this man a lot of money these past months, and we both understood that neither of us would see each other again. Despite being a flashy, pretentious, high-profile lawyer, he was an honorable man. I knew he would do everything possible to speed up the corrupt and cumbersome Greek system. Briefly, I wondered how much of that seven thousand the judge actually got. I was sure my lawyer got most of it. He always did. I put that thought out of my mind. I was hugely excited about being released, but I would not allow myself to believe it until it happened.

Over the next couple of days, I waited for someone to call me. When nothing happened, and the hours and days slipped by, disappointment crept in. My emotional pendulum swung back the other way, and my spirits started to sink. I was completely exhausted. I started to think that the idea of walking out of this place was only a dream. It was July 12th, and it had been five days since my lawyer came to see me and three weeks since the judge said I could get out.

My God! What if Stephanie was right? What if I had been conned again? The thought of that hurt too much...no way could I have misjudged so badly. But it kept at me: "Michael, what have you done now?"

I was talking with Mario in the main corridor on this morning when a skinny Arab man approched. I stepped back and tensed. He excused himself and said "Captain, mister wants to speak with you. Please come with me."

I looked at him, and back at Mario, who just gave me a blank look.

"Listen. I do not know who you are, and I do not know mister. I do not want any trouble. I just want to be left alone."

"You don't understand," the man replied. "Mister needs to speak with the captain."

I glared at him. "Why don't you come back later? Right now, I'm busy." He nodded and scampered back down the cellblock corridor.

Mario asked me if I knew who that was. I had no clue. He told me that was the lackey for the Egyptian. "I have been in this place for three years," Mario said. "I have never seen him. He is doing life for murder and never comes out of his cell. He lives in the very last cell at the end of the main corridor."

"Why in the hell does he want to speak to me?" I wondered. I was very worried, thinking it might have something to do with The Manga. That sick feeling came over me. I just wanted to be invisible and get out of here. I wondered for an instant if I would ever see my home again.

When the cells opened that evening, I stepped out. Looking up at the three stories of concrete-enclosed humanity, I moaned deep inside, knowing that I was losing everything and everyone I loved and there was nothing I could do to stop it.

The skinny Arab, as promised, approached. I stopped him a few feet away and asked, "Am I in danger?"

He replied in his broken English, "Of course not, Captain. Mister sees something in your future, and he must tell you." He turned and started back down the long corridor, so I followed. I stood outside the last cell on the very end of the cellblock's main floor.

The skinny Arab stepped inside, and I could feel a few pairs of eyes on me, probably wondering what the crazy American was up to now. I wondered that myself as I walked in, ready to bolt if anything came at me. It was very dark, except for a soft glow of light next to the gaunt Arab who motioned for me to sit. I could see the bottom bunk had a curtain cover, and I could tell someone was inside. A thought echoed in my head, "What the hell am I doing in here?"

"Mister is a seer," the man began. "His mother was a seer.

His grandmother was a seer, and so was his great grandmother."

"Excuse me for being so stupid," I said. "But I have no idea what a seer is."

"Mister can see things in the future for certain people," he replied. "Why the hell me?" I asked. "I don't know him, and he doesn't know me."

The curtain opened, and I stood up, startled. I was looking at a young boy dressed in a silky, black Arab gown. For some reason, the silly thought crossed my mind that an Arab only needed a few different colored gowns and he would have an entire wardrobe. But I was surprised and showed it. He could not have been any older than eighteen, thin with a slight build and completely black eyes. I mean black! His pupils, the whites of his eyes, everything pure black. Strangest eyes I have ever seen. He said something in Arabic. His lackey translated, telling me I have *chi*.

I snapped back. "No, I don't! I don't even know what chi is!"

He said something to Mister, and they laughed a kind of weird soundless laugh. "Chi is a powerful energy. Mister says you have it." He stated.

I said nothing, sitting there in the dark, trying to make sense of why I was here.

They continued and told me two things that stuck with me: One, I would be leaving this place very soon. Two, the number three was very good for me and I was to remember that. About half an hour had passed, and I was getting restless. I stood and thanked them both. Mister just raised his hand in a good-bye gesture.

As I took a step toward the door, he said something else, which was translated. "Captain, Mister says your problems do not end here. Be careful at home. You will have trouble there." The gaunt Arab cautioned me.

I looked sharply at this Mister kid with the weird black eyes and hippy, dippy serenity and irritating little smirk. Shaking my head, I turned back and stepped out of the darkness into the lighted corridor, heading toward my end of the cellblock. "What the hell was that?" I said out loud to myself. "Michael, you're starting to crack! You've got to get out of here!"

I spotted Lefteri waving me over. "You have spoken to the Egyptian?" he asked in a serious direct tone.

"Yeah, he's a young kid with very weird eyes," I replied.

"Michael, this Egyptian is strong and has a power," Lefteri said. "I have been in here seven years and have not said a word to him. And he's in his forties."

My mouth dropped." No way! Now that is spooky."

"I *will* see you tomorrow," Lefteri said as a matter of fact, with the emphasis on the word *will*.

I did not understand what he meant until the following day. It was almost lockdown time, but I wanted to stop and tell Mario about the Egyptian. I thought he would find my story amusing, but on the contrary, he was worried for me, cautioning me to step lightly.

Although I was anxious about how much longer I would be here, Mario knew I would be leaving soon. "Remember the day you cleaned the cats from the boiler room?" he asked.

"Not one of my shining moments." I replied.

"Just the opposite," Mario said. "Before that day, you were our friend. After that day, you became our hero. We were proud to be your friends."

Glancing at his face, I saw that he was serious. Standing next to him were the small Italians, nodding their heads and smiling. They knew exactly what Mario had just said to me. I stood next to my friend, staring straight ahead, and said nothing.

"Captain," he continued, "you have to tell them what is going on in here! Somehow you must let people know."

"I'll try, Mario," I answered. "But who would believe me without witnessing it themselves?"

He just shrugged.

"Like the tree in the forest that makes no sound when it falls if nobody is in the forest to hear it," I said.

He turned and smiled at me, his face kind and understanding. In a soft, almost philosophical tone, he continued, "Captain, we have talked together every day for many months. I have learned what kind of man you are and have witnessed your character." He tilted his head and spoke slowly. "It is important for me to tell you how much your friendship has meant to me. You gave me strength and hope without even realizing it."

I stood next to my small friend, not speaking but knowing he was talking for both of us. I put my arm around his sagging shoulders as he let out a sigh. Next to Mario were his two loyal friends, leaning forward and staring at their friend with sad eyes, mimicking his movements as he spoke to me.

I enjoyed listening to Mario speak English with his eloquent accent as he said, "Captain, this morning I understood I will never have your company again for the rest of my life. I have told you all about where I come from. How much I cherish my mama and papa, and every detail about my brothers and sisters."

"I know Mario, I feel like I know them and have developed a strong fondness for your entire family," I replied with a genuine smile in my voice.

Still looking down, he spoke slightly louder, "I know nothing about you except your name, and even then, I've always thought I should call you Captain. You have not spoken about your family or where you grew up. You have not volunteered anything personal about yourself." With insistence he said, "Now I feel I must know something about you and where you come from."

I stood stiff, staring straight ahead at nothing particular. A quick thought came to me. "You're absolutely right, Mario," I exclaimed. "Since the beginning of my lockup inside these foreign prisons, I have spoken very little about my family and the people I love."

129

Cautiously, I tried to explain. "I believed that if I talked about them inside these horrible places, I would be exposing them to this terrible human existence. I convinced myself that in some strange or mystical way they would feel my pain and loneliness. I could not take that chance!"

Neither of us spoke for several minutes. My thoughts became hard and deep, thinking about what happens to men locked inside such hopeless and forsaken places like these lost prisons. A human instinct surfaces, and the need for another person's trust and friendship becomes strong.

Sometimes a bond can develop that can be far stronger than anything you could experience on the outside. I had tried to avoid that pitfall, but despite my hardness I knew a camaraderie had grown with my good Italian friend. I cared about him very much!

Breaking the long silence, I spoke, "We come from very similar backgrounds, but from different parts of the world. Like you, I was raised in a modest, loving family with two older brothers, two younger sisters, and my twin sister and I were in the middle. I have a specific love for each one of my brothers and sisters. Many memories have come to me while being in lockdown, but the foremost thing I remember is always feeling proud to be a part of my family."

Feeling as if I was talking to myself, I continued, "My father was a good man, a master sergeant in the U.S. Marine Corps. I liked his strength and discipline and tried to apply it to my academics and athletics. My mother was exceptional. While raising six children, she made each of us feel as if we were her only child. I have always had a special bond with my mother, and I know she has that same specialness for me. This past year I have come to know deep loneliness and despair. Those emotions don't compare with the terror and panic I have experienced when thinking I might never see or speak to my mother again!"

I stopped talking, and felt Mario looking up at me. I whispered, "I've got to get home!"

The next morning, when the cells opened, I wanted to just lose a day, forget I was here. I could hear the cellblock loudspeaker in the background but could not understand what they were saying.

Suddenly Mario rushed in, shouting at me that they were calling my name and telling me to get my ass up to the cell gates. I jumped up, grabbing my knapsack. Mario was out the door, telling me to hurry up. I did not have anything, did not want anything from this place. I think I did about four complete turns before I got out the cell door, my heart racing as I ran the football field length of the corridor to the cellblock gates. My God, what if it was a nasty trick by someone, and they were going to laugh and tell me, "Sorry!"

The guards were motioning for me to hurry. No way was I staying behind now. I stopped at the gates and turned around, trying to find my good friend Mario. I saw his face fifty feet from me off to the side. I looked at his kind moist eyes, big smile, and saw a face that was genuinely happy for me. I also knew my other friends were watching me go from a distance, saying their own good-byes. The few that had gotten to know me understood I would think of them, but that I would never look back.

When I looked into Mario's eyes, I had to choke down mixed emotions of pain and joy at getting out of this place. My dear friend Mario would have to survive twelve more years inside this terrible place.

Watching me go had to hurt in a way that would stay with him a long time. With my eyes, I told him I would think of him for the rest of my life. I watched him put both his hands on his heart, his way of saying good-bye. My body stiffened with purpose and I sent him my strongest American salute. I turned and walked through the cellblock gates. Not looking back, the guards escorted me to the next lockdown. The pain and heartache I felt would be put aside, thought about later. I needed to get myself home first. Mario knew this.

16

The clang of the prison gates did not sound as ominous going out as they had coming in. The door to the last office opened, and I was greeted with a giant smile and the serious eyes of my mentor, protector, and dear friend, Lefteri. The irony was perfect. Of course, he would be the last person I would see before getting out. I gripped his shoulders and hugged him, telling him how rewarding it had been for me to have him pass through my life. Over the past months, I had learned how much of a strong, principled, good man he was. I could tell Lefteri was a little excited. He was sincerely happy to see me getting out.

He spoke in his usual precise manner, "Michael, you taught me many things."

I couldn't help but say, "Right! How to be a good idiot in a bad place."

"You can never take a compliment without making one of your usually not-very-funny jokes," he said, laughing. "You have something I would like to have."

"Anything, anything you want," I answered.

He just shook his head. "No, no, Michael. In this place, I can only imagine your frustration at not being able to communicate with words. The hostile prison environment teaches a man where he measures and how he fits. You measure very high. Your unassuming presence combined with your huge confidence speaks for you. It is a curiosity that attracts people. This is what you have that I would like."

As we shook hands, I realized that he was the kind of man who always got the better grip. One of those rare men who never waste words. Everything he said always had substance to it. His last words to me, I knew, had been spoken for both of us.

"Thank you, my good friend," he said. Then his voice dropped, and he whispered one more thing, "Do not take an airplane." A look of surprise crossed my face, but I saw the smile in his eyes and said nothing.

Without ceremony, the guard opened a simple wooden door that led to the world outside. Excitement and nerves had me feeling slightly paranoid. I was standing on the side of a busy dirt road on a blistering hot Athens morning. It was July thirteenth, and despite my confusion, I wondered if this is what the mysterious Egyptian meant by my lucky number three.

A year ago, almost to the day, I had been taken from a life of wide-open freedom that only being a captain on the world's oceans can provide, to a place so opposite and sinister, I had never imagined it existed. A place where a man's self-worth, self-respect, and dignity is peeled away, layer by layer, in an effort to take his soul. With some men, they fail.

The emotional shock I experienced as I stepped out of that degrading existence was only matched by the elation I felt. I wished I could share this natural high with someone I loved. Once again, I suppressed my feelings. I needed to focus on how to get home.

Walking the streets of this congested, claustrophobic city woke up my senses. I was on maximum alert, and the constant movement of thousands of people, along with the noise created by every car honking its horn, hurt in a way that actually felt good. I knew Athens and the surrounding countryside, having spent a lot of time here back in the '80s. The sounds and smells were becoming familiar again, despite my disorientation.

Getting on a bus and making my way south to the seaside town of Glyfada where I used to live was the first step in the plan, I had spent so much time thinking about. I had to get out of this country without taking an airplane. Lefteri knew what I had planned.

Customs at the airport might still have me on an Interpol red flag alert. I figured I had three days to get out before someone from the police might come looking for me.

If they thought I was going hang around waiting for an appeal, they had to be nuts. Breaking the conditions of my early release would bring them looking for me and send me back to prison. Deep inside, I was not sure if I would allow myself to go back to that existence. I do know a side of me would make a good argument against it. I was on the run!

Standing in the middle of the bus, packed like sardines, I held onto the worn leather strap hanging from the top. I looked at everyone moving together as the old bus popped and chugged its way south along the coast. The jerking and swaying almost seemed choreographed.

I fell into a sort of trance, feeling euphoric about just being released, free of the prisons that had stolen a year of my life. Because of the way this day had started and what it had already shown me, I knew I would be able to reflect back and recognize it as one of the most powerful days of my life.

It was about noon and boiling hot when I got off the bus in Glyfada. The prison had provided me with about twenty-five dollars in Greek drachmas—not a lot—but it would get me through the day until I could organize a wire transfer. I had things to arrange before I called Stephanie. I had to be able to tell her what I needed for my plan to work.

That night, the town square was packed when I went looking for a pay telephone to call home. God! I was loving it as I walked around, soaking it all up like a dry sponge. Except when I saw a policeman...then panic and anxiety would urge me to get the hell out of sight.

A simple thing like using a telephone without a cellblock full of outlaws breathing down your neck suddenly became one of life's luxuries. I picked up the pay phone in the middle of the square, excited to make the call. No one at home knew I had been released.

The news would spread fast to family and friends, including the yachting community of Fort Lauderdale. So many of those people had been incredibly supportive. I could not wait to thank them all.

Her familiar soft voice said, "Hello?"

"Stephanie" I said, excited. "I'm standing in the town square." I looked up, my voice cracking, "I haven't seen a night sky in a year!" We were both crying. "Don't worry about any of that other stuff at home. I understand. We can work things out for the best."

I gave her the bank transfer details I had arranged that day, telling her of my plan and explaining that things had to be followed precisely. Finally, reluctantly, I had to let her go. "Good-bye, I'll see you in a few days." Her last words filled me with a surge of affection. "Michael, I love you. Be careful!" I thought for sure that I could float across the street.

The stark little hotel room I rented had stiff white sheets that felt like cardboard covering a small single bed. Even so, I felt like I was staying at the Ritz. I was exhausted, but my mind would not shut down. I have planned many trips and long voyages across oceans, and rarely does one go perfectly. Usually, it is human error or neglect that sends it off the rails. I could not afford for this plan to be derailed. Unfortunately, it would depend to a great degree on human performance and a lot of luck to get me home.

Stephanie and my family and friends never knew the deal I had made with the Greek court. I had paid a judge to grant me early release. No foreign inmate was ever granted this. The conditions of the court were expected to be followed, which meant I could not have my passport back, and I would be denied exit from Greece and arrested again if I tried to leave. I had assured the judge and court that I would stay in Greece and wait for my appeal. Now I was about to take a huge gamble with my life.

If I had to stay in prison for another year, I would wind up dead or mentally destroyed. So, really, it was not a gamble to me. I just had to get out.

Stephanie accomplished the first step by swiftly wiring me money to the bank I had arranged an account with. Because of the ten-hour time difference, I collected my money first thing in the morning and was on my way to the American Embassy in downtown Athens.

The Greek court had kept my passport, so I was very worried about how I would be received at the embassy. I was hoping to reach the right person and tell the exact truth about what I was doing. They had no obligation to issue me a new passport, and I was not even sure they could because they were obliged to follow Greek law. I also knew if they said they could issue one, I had to somehow convince them to do it today. The anxiety rose as I began my Mission Impossible.

My stomach was in big knots as the taxi pulled up to the embassy gate, but only three hours later I had that prized document in my hand. With the little blue book and a giant grin on my face, I practically skipped out the embassy entrance. I could not stop myself from giving the U.S. Marine guard a salute along with a sincere, "Thank you."

On the sidewalk outside the embassy, I stopped to absorb the kindness the people inside had shown me. They had treated me as if I were famous: shaking my hand, showing concern about my welfare. They told me the ambassador's office had received dozens of letters from around the world, all voicing their support for me. A little self-confidence kicked in just by having normal conversations again.

It occurred to me that the wonderful hospitality and conversation I had enjoyed with the embassy people was magnified because of how drastically opposite it was to what I had been living with this past year. I also could not help but notice that a couple of the embassy personnel who had been liaisons for my family and supporters were slightly embarrassed at their inability to do much at all for me while I was in Korydallos.

It was not their fault. The U.S.A. does not have a mandate to help its citizens in real trouble abroad. But I also sensed that, in the beginning, both the American Consulate in Turkey and the American Embassy here in Greece automatically thought I must have deserved what happened to me. As the overwhelming International support became evident, these people were now doing all they could to help me. Even bending the rules, a little. For this, I was grateful.

My new passport, by law, had a paper attached stating that my original passport was being held by the Greek authorities and this was a temporary document. I promptly ripped that off! This was my ticket home, not out of Greece, but through customs in Italy. I still planned to leave Greece without taking the chance of showing my passport. It would be difficult, but I hoped I would get a break.

The confusion in the huge main bus terminal in downtown Athens was overwhelming. I struggled to stay focused, managing to find the bus leaving for the Port of Patra. I bought a ticket for the seven-hour, overnight ride to the far west point of the Peloponnesus region of Greece. This is where the ferries left for their trip across the Adriatic Sea to the east coast of Italy.

The bus ride was tortuous—it was not exactly a greyhound, more like an old school bus. It rumbled through the pitch-black night across the Greek countryside. I got no sleep but did not care. It was a pleasure to watch the sun coming up just as we reached the port.

Patra is busy twenty-four hours a day, so I went in search of the ferries sailing to Ancona, Italy. Through the years, I had been to this city several times, so it did not take me long to find the two ships traveling to Ancona. I stood off the perimeter of one that was scheduled to leave that morning. They were busy loading goods and supplies and had a line of trucks waiting to go on. This was it. I had to decide whether to go through customs or sneak on and avoid a passport check. I was getting that awful panicky feeling in my stomach, something I seemed to have lived with a very long time.

Still glancing around, I had no idea what I was looking for, when suddenly I spotted them. I walked right up to the two men sitting at a taverna table outside. They both had big cold bottles of Amstel beer.

"Those look good," I said. "Mind if I join you for a few minutes? I'm waiting for the ferry to Ancona."

"American, right?" one of them asked, saying they were English.

I nodded, and they both smiled, welcoming me to sit down.

It was not even nine o'clock in the morning, but it had to be at least eighty-five degrees out. The English guys were setting a good pace. They kept count by keeping the empty bottles on the table. I was tense and nervous but enjoyed myself in their company. Taking a deep breath, I told them my story, flat out straight. They stopped sipping their beer for a few minutes as they listened. Their interest was obvious. They stared at me and asked questions, the answers to which produced some shocked looks.

Finally, we stood up. They were ready to load their truck, and I needed to move over by the ship's passport control so I could find out if they were using the computer for checks. If I had no choice but to go through, there was no question that I was ready to bolt. I would at least make them work to catch me.

One of the Englishmen suggested I hide in their truck, and the other one quickly agreed, saying they never checked inside. I know the appreciation showed in my eyes.

"That would be just great, you guys! Thanks," I said. It was not much considering what they were doing for me, but I could tell they wanted to help. One of them had suggested earlier that I was probably on some CIA mission anyway. The nervous tension that controlled my body every minute of every day certainly made me feel like I was.

Later, my eyes snapped open, not groggy with sleep but with wakefulness. I was in the back of the Englishmen's big semi, down in the ferry's garage. Something had startled me awake. After a moment, I realized it was the silence. The familiar noises of the cellblock that I had lived with for the past year were just a memory.

I made my way up through the ship's insides and stepped out onto the open top deck. Instinctively, I glanced around, feeling the roll of the ship and knowing we were at sea. There was no land in sight. I was out of Greece!

In a trance, I clenched the forward handrail, my knuckles white with the intensity of my grip. The sky was crystal clear, a blue that was the one and only true *blue*. This sky, this day, defined the color. The giant orange ball going down over the flat, calm water looked so close it appeared to be the ship's destination.

So many years at sea, and I had never really looked at the oceans I had sailed upon. Never let them inside me. Never felt them penetrate my soul. Never fully appreciated the ultimate freedom they had given me like I did at that moment.

My mind fought off the emotion that threatened to buckle my knees. "Not yet, Michael," I was whispering to myself. "Get home, get yourself home."

An English voice behind me—which for some reason always sounds hilarious to me—said, "For Christ's sakes mate, with that look, you'd think you haven't seen a bloody sunset in a year!"

I burst out with a laugh that made me choke. I could not stop. Kneeling on the deck, I felt like something had broken inside and it all came out.

They were laughing at me not being able to stop laughing. Jokingly, one said, "Come on, mate, it wasn't that funny. You're embarrassing us!" They lifted me up, stuck a beer in my hand, and we guided each other to the bar.

The overnight ferry docked in Ancona, Italy, the next morning. I needed an entry stamp in my passport, and I chose to risk it here at the ferries because they were much more lax than the airport in Rome. Walking toward passport control, my gut churning, I passed through without incident.

As the train rattled toward Rome, I kept thinking I was on the third leg of my four-point plan to get home: bus, ferry, train, and plane. I gave the job of having a plane ticket waiting for me in Rome to my sister Doris. I knew she would make sure it was there. A strong lady with the least to give...in the clutch, she would give the most.

I was picturing my English pals rumbling up Europe toward England. They had come briefly into my life for a reason. I had a need, and they fulfilled it without any conditions. Just as quickly as they had entered my life, they had gotten back on the track of their own. I knew they would tell the story about the American CIA captain to their friends in the pub at home.

Nervous paranoia and driving discipline kept my personal celebration in check. I kept telling myself to wait; it was not time yet. *Not yet, you are not home yet.* I would realize much later that these two controls had become embedded deep inside my personality. It took a while, with the help of a couple of people, to soften their sharp edges.

I checked into a small motel in Rome I had stayed in several years before and made the call to my sister. I told her to get me on the first flight to New York or any American city on the East Coast. When I hung up with her, I made one more call, to the American Embassy in Rome. After being on hold several times, I spoke to the right person. I explained my situation, saying I was worried I would be red flagged by Interpol for something that I had already been arrested for. He was a nice guy, and we talked for a few minutes. He even offered to meet me at the airport. I paused, thinking that was interesting, wondering what he was thinking. I declined, hoping it would not be necessary. Hanging up, I was glad

I had at least made a contact at the embassy. When I called her back, Doris had arranged a flight for me the next day.

I hardly slept that night, knowing that, once again, I would have to pass through a checkpoint. The next morning, I went through the Rome airport's passport control. Despite my tension and fear, I passed through, and I was on my last leg, the airplane flying across the Atlantic.

I thought I should treat myself to a beer, but truthfully, I only had a couple of sips with the English guys. I had not drunk any alcohol for a very long time, and it didn't taste that good. Besides, I told myself to wait until I got all the way home; perhaps it would taste better.

On the long flight to New York, it was a constant battle to keep the serious thoughts and emotions at bay. I just wanted to feel light instead of the heaviness I carried inside me. I was certain touching American soil would shed some of the weight. I came through customs at JFK, at last realizing I was really back in America! I did not kiss the ground or go through any kind of ritual, but I was elated. I hurried through the terminals to get my connecting flight to Fort Lauderdale and home.

Already I could feel that awful paranoia starting to fade. I was almost there. Later, down the road, I might think about the experience and the emotional roller coaster I had been on for the past five days getting myself back, but not now.

17

My plane touched down in Fort Lauderdale. I was not sure of the reception I would have. My sister had given Stephanie the flight details, but I had not talked with her since that first night, five long days ago, in the little town square. I had no luggage, just a small beat-up knapsack.

The three of them were waiting when I came off the plane. My good friends, Paul and Jeanne, were with Stephanie. The girls screamed and wrapped their arms around me. Paul shook my hand. A great feeling broke through the ice of uncertainty. I hugged Stephanie tightly in an embrace that said everything. Suddenly, nothing that had happened between us mattered to me. I cared for her, no matter what.

"We'll find our lives again. I made it. Thank you, darlin'," I whispered.

Her reply of, "Michael, I'm so proud of you," made my heart jump!

That first night home was a bit of a blur. Seeing the dozens of yellow ribbons on the front lawn, even on the neighbors' houses, startled me a little. It did not register that they were for me. I had dreamed of this moment a thousand times, but I was drained and could not say much. As we pulled into the driveway, my front door opened, and everyone poured out with cheers and greetings.

I think it was supposed to be a surprise, but my friend Gus could not contain himself. It was truly one of the best nights of my life, full of laughs, drinks, hugs, and kisses!

The first few day's home were wonderful, but difficult. Thankfully, Stephanie and I seemed to slip into an unspoken arrangement. We were waiting to see what happened before deciding anything. Life came back to me in a flood, but I am sure I appeared anxious and tense. Some media wanted interviews; I received many calls and saw many people. I wanted to say thankyou to everyone, but I could not relax. The only thing I really wanted was to get back to work.

I was stunned to learn how many people had supported me and how much they had given. It made me uneasy. I felt vulnerable and seemed incapable of thanking everyone.

The one person I wanted and needed to see most was my boss and friend, Mr. R. His support, both emotionally and monetarily, had been extraordinary. His loyalty had given me the credibility that saved my career. When thinking of people that have been in my life, without doubt he has taught and influenced me more than anyone else.

I was nervous and apprehensive when I arrived at the large business complex owned by Mr. R. I worried that I would not be able to convey to him how much his friendship and support meant to me and my family. I was overwhelmed with his personal greeting at the main door. His commanding charisma swallowed me up as he put his arm over my shoulder and guided me through the maze of offices. I could feel his pride swell at watching me receive an almost celebrity welcome from all his employees. The warm reception I was given made me feel a huge sense of gratitude. He invited me into his executive office with genuine graciousness. Our conversation was warm and caring, and I could feel his familiar presence and his sincere friendship fill the room.

He ended our meeting by motivating me like only he could. He locked onto my eyes with his and said, "Michael, in the jungle out there, you are truly one of the lions."

After being home a week, my inability to concentrate and focus on more than one thing at a time was getting frustrating. It brought out my anger, and I caught myself thinking a few times that I would love someone to just look at me cross-eyed. I was not really aware of the hardness I had brought home with me. Looking back, I can recognize the restless intensity I carried around. It was noticed by the people who were close to me, and it concerned them. Someone later told me I walked around smoldering. It took a long time for me to understand just how much.

Stephanie and I were friendly and respectful with each other but in no way had we been intimate since I got back. Honestly, neither of us felt like it. Who knows the reasons? But we had a strong bond and had developed a partnership over the years. I knew I was not any good at repairing relationships. I spent little time thinking about this and even less time doing anything about it.

I did not want, and certainly did not enjoy, the notoriety and attention I was receiving. It seemed to me that a few people had become caught up with it. The welcome-home parties were appreciated, but it soon made me uncomfortable. I needed to be left alone and just get back to work, doing what I used to do.

Hellish Nightmare Over For M/Y "Picante" Captain!

"I would either still be there or dead if it wasn't for Stephanie. Her unbelievable tenacity love and devotion saved me." These were Michael's first words when I sat down and talked with him.

It was a twenty minute notice. That's all Michael Churchward was given. A notice from a fellow inmate named Lefterios that ran the prison computers. A notice that he was being released to go home after one year of being in prison not in one but two countries. A notice from a man who Michael says taught him how to survive in a maximum security general population prison

Welcome home Captain Churchward

with about 1700 inmates . "There is no worse place on earth."

Michael, who has been traveling the Mediterranean for many years captaining some of the busiest charter yachts was running the 120' "Picante" when his nightmare began. After leaving Mykonos and pulling into a port in Turkey where they had been several times already that season, Michael had been told by local authorities upon checking in , that there was a problem with his passport and he needed to come to the station. Not fearing anything, a having ships papers and everything in order and having gone through security checks in many countries over the past several years, he couldn't imagine he had any problem, least of all from a previous employer he had only argued with and had not bothered to file a police report of any kind back in 1991, nor has there been an investigation done to this day, which he found out much later. Michael was held 90 days before he even found out what the charges were. "I should have gotten into the tender and took off." But thinking of his crew and Yacht he followed what he thought was the right decision.

During this time Michael sat in a Turkish prison not knowing what events were taking place. For Stephanie Moor the nightmare was all to real. Still in Turkey confused and not knowing what the charges were she began to get caught up in a web of lies and extorsion attempts from all types of individuals that thought they could make a buck. Many times this amounted to several thousands of dollars for phony promises. "It was the system and those involved in it, not the everyday people." said Stephanie. "I found the people on the streets, the cab drivers, the shop owners, the local yachting community and all the people who knew Michael for years could not believe what was happening. Yet they also were helpless." The Michael Churchward story headlined the Turkish press. One newspaper showed Stephanie in tears after she was told in the court that Michael would not be released.

"The Turkish press was very sympathetic in fact. There articles became more and more critical of what they were

First night home at my front door in Fort Lauderdale, FL with Stephanie.

18

I had been home three weeks when it happened. About ten in the evening, I started to worry. Stephanie was not home yet, and that was very unusual. Suddenly, I felt the hair stand up on my neck, and those lousy butterflies were back in my stomach. I knew.

I got dressed and drove down to the marina where the small boat Stephanie had been working on was moored. Her car was parked to the side, so I started down the weathered dock, the sound of creaky boards breaking the dead silence of the warm night. The light was dim as I boarded the boat and knocked on the side door. Through the window, I could see a light coming from the stateroom below. I knocked louder, and a minute later, Stephanie appeared, coming up the stairs into the main salon. She could see me through the door window but did not open it right away. She was wearing a white sun dress and her hair was a bit disheveled. She avoided looking me in the eyes. Speaking through the door, she said, "Michael, just go home. I will be home in a few minutes. I have to finish cleaning the stateroom bathrooms."

I responded with a deep, angry voice, "Stephanie, open the fucking door!"

She fumbled with the lock, finally getting it open. Her eyes were still fixed on the carpet as I stepped inside.

The anguish could be heard in my voice when I asked, "Stephanie, what are you doing?" She looked up with trembling lips and tears filling her eyes, but before she could answer, another figure appeared behind her, slowly coming up the stairs from below. He had no shirt on, just a pair of boxer shorts.

Of course, this was the man she was having her affair with, a neighbor from some apartments a few doors down.

I did not know him, but three days before, looking out my front door and watching Stephanie cross the street with her dog Max, I had seen him duck behind a house with his own dog. I instantly knew this was Lover Boy. The same Lover Boy who now had his arms straight out, holding a gun in some kind of fucking two-handed police stance, pointed right at my chest.

Realizing what I had interrupted, I turned to look at Steph. I was not pissed about her affair. I had gotten past that a few days after she told me back in prison. She could not bring herself to look at my face and see the profound disappointment over her deception and lies. She knew this was something I could never tolerate.

Stephanie turned, startled at seeing the gun, and screamed at him, "Get the hell out of here!" At the same time, she tried to get me back on the dock, pleading, "Let's just go home and talk this through, Michael."

In another time, another place, common sense might have prevailed. But not this time, not this place. Excitement and adrenaline flooded me so fast, it was the most incredible rush! My body tightened like steel, and every one of my senses, every nerve ending, felt razor sharp. God! It was crazy; it was awesome. I could tell I had a grin on my face, my eyes narrowing. Slipping into that zone felt GREAT!

This is why my friends were concerned. They had tried to talk to me about the seething anger and tightness I had been carrying around with me since I got home. I had not been able to see it and had just shrugged them off.

Suddenly, I realized I wanted this! I needed this! And, there was not anyone more perfect than this punk with the gun for me to explode on. He saw the grin on my face, and in an unsure, nervous voice, threatened to blow my head off.

I knew Lover Boy had imagined this moment would come. The idea of being face-to-face with someone who had just been released from prison, let alone the mystique of having been in a hard-core Turkish lockdown, had him terrified. He knew fighting me toe-to-toe was absolutely out of the question.

He felt he would need a gun, and to be honest, if I were him, looking at me at this moment, I would have thought the same thing. But it was my guess he had been carrying the gun around with him since the day I got home!

The three of us made it onto the dock with the asshole still pointing his gun at me with both hands, ready to fire. My anger reached a peak as he came closer, ignoring Stephanie's pleas. I do not remember all the things I said, but I know I told him at the top of my lungs that he should have brought a whole fucking arsenal.

Taunting his chicken-shit ass, I asked, "Aren't you man enough to face me, toe-to-toe? Talk to me, tell me the situation, and deal with the consequences. That's what real MEN do!"

He said nothing, but he understood he was being exposed for the punk he was. Judging by the look on his face, he also knew he would have to shoot me to stop me. My gaze was infrared, piercing right through him, and he flinched. Suddenly I saw it in his face. He had decided he was going to fire that 9 mm.

For some reason, there is an extra sense that develops in a person who spends time in a maximum-security lockdown. I had developed this sense, and it told me he was going to shoot me. I jumped him without warning, covering the five feet separating us and landed a vicious shove to his chest that caught him unprepared. He had no chance to regain his footing on the edge of the wood planks and fell backward into the black water. His reaction—bringing the gun up with both hands, aiming to kill—made me recoil.

The deafening sounds of two loud bangs broke the silent night. I had been right, the son of a bitch really wanted to end my life.

A powerful silence followed, as one of the bullets raced into the darkness, and the second one found Stephanie. I felt her limp body slump next to me.

Kneeling, I saw the scared look on her face. She whispered just a single word with a question: "Michael?"

The blood gushing from her started to soak the beautiful white sun dress she was wearing. My heart skipped and fear gripped me. "You bastard!" I yelled at this punk. I scooped her up without effort and ran to my truck. Racing through the streets, I kept talking to her, "Come on, Steph. Hang on, darlin'. You'll be okay."

I ran into the emergency room, yelling for someone to help us. Several people came out of nowhere, taking her from me. She lay on the gurney, and I held her hand while sharp scissors quickly cut off her dress. People feverishly worked around her. The swollen purple hole on the side of her hip was hideous. It struck me just how much of a personal violation a bullet penetrating flesh really is.

Transfixed, my mind seemed to clearly see my experiences of this past year, right up to this moment. Did I really live it? Did I survive the emotional extremes, or had it left scars? I was furious at seeing Stephanie hurt. I was furious that a punk with a gun, who knew nothing, had done nothing, had been nowhere in life, in an instant, could have such a shattering impact on others. It seemed that this had been the year that more than just a few of these people had crossed my path. People with such badness in them. People I never knew existed. Seeking out other's misfortunes and looking for ways to benefit or profit. They all took a chunk, a bite, a pound of flesh, stretching my emotional boundaries beyond repair. This had taken its toll, leaving me with an anger frozen deep inside that would stay with me a long, long time.

Someone was pulling me away as they pushed her down the hall through the swinging doors. I could hear her soft cries. She kept saying over and over, "Michael, I'm so sorry! I'm so sorry." I stood still, paralyzed. Slowly, I bent down and picked up the blood-soaked dress, staring me right in the face was the label that read "SIZE 3." THE EGYPTIAN! The seer had said my lucky number was three. Did it mean the start of a better year? It occurred to me that it could not be much worse.

'Not only did she single-handedly get me out of prison, now she's taken a bullet for me. My God, I can deal with all that other stuff.'

MICHAEL CHURCHWARD

BOB EIGHMIE / Herald Staff

STILL IN LOVE: Former prisoner Michael Churchward and his girlfriend, Stephanie Morr.

Relationship survives prison ordeal, gunfire

By DAVID KIDWELL
Herald Staff Writer

After a year of living in the stench of sewage and sleeping on the concrete floors of Turkish and Greek prisons, facing charges he knew were false, Michael Churchward's Fort Lauderdale homecoming was supposed to be all hugs, champagne and airport banners.

Instead, it marked the end of one tragedy halfway around the world and the beginning of another closer to home.

Churchward's fiancee, Stephanie Morr — whose unrelenting worldwide campaign to free him enlisted Dustin Hoffman and H. Ross Perot — had turned to another man for solace.

The relationship, she says, was born out of despair. It ended last week with an angry confrontation and a gunshot that has left Morr temporarily in a wheelchair.

"It was the ultimate betrayal, I know that," said Morr, 37, crying — and lamenting her relationship with David Oliver Fraser, 33. "I knew Michael was all alone over there, and I'll always have that guilt.

19

Stephanie's injury was severe. The bullet shattered her hip and the road to recovery was long, painful, and tortuous at times. After a significant hospital stay, I brought her home to my house in Fort Lauderdale.

Needless to say, my return home made local headlines. But after the shooting, the media became overwhelming. National networks, cable news, and TV shows like *Inside Edition*, *20/20*, and *Dateline* all wanted us to sign and do programs with them. Writing books, making movies, all kinds of BS was coming at us. I wanted none of it. All I wanted was to care for Stephanie and try to get some part of my life back.

She was bedridden, and it took months before she was able to stand and walk on her own. During that time, she needed me, and without question, I believed It was my turn to look after her. I told myself she had been under incredible pressure this past year and was very vulnerable. Who the hell cared about an affair! She took a bullet for me! I owed her!

The past year had taken an enormous toll on both of us. It became apparent I was not the same man she had sailed around the world with. Focus and sleep were luxuries. Anger and anxiety were seething just below the surface. My adjustment to being home was far more difficult than I imagined. I severely underestimated the impact and damage those brutal foreign prisons had on my mental and physical well-being.

Immediately after the shooting, we were contacted by detectives and ultimately the local prosecutor's office. They informed us that an aggressive case was being put together against the shooter.

Indictment and prosecution were inevitable, and they wanted to know if we were prepared and willing to go through a very tough and public trial. My response was perhaps a little too much of an angry and enthusiastic yes. Stephanie looked at me with an exhausted and deeply hurt look in her eyes, giving the prosecutor a slow and reluctant nod.

Mr. R called weekly without fail, always asking how we were doing. In retrospect, I understood his sharp and intent manner was taking measure on how I was handling the circumstances. After several months, he finally asked me the question I had been hoping for: "Michael, I would like you to take back command of *Picante*. She is due in port soon, and I have many plans in mind and I need you, if you are willing and feel up to it."

My excitement was transparent. I tried to calm myself, containing the adrenaline surging inside as I answered quietly, "I would be honored, sir." Remembering with clarity a dark time not long ago where I was incapable of imagining this day, I said to myself, "Yes, the pendulum is beginning to swing back my way."

The news and my excitement at being back on board spread throughout the yachting community. I reached out for a couple of capable and reliable old crew that brought with them a professional pride along with a shared gratitude at being back together as shipmates.

Picante soon started to feel and look beautiful again. A few weeks passed, and with a subdued excitement, Mr. R. revealed his plan. He wanted me to go down under to western Australia and survey a vessel he was interested in buying. Depending on the condition I found this ship in, I would commence an entire rebuild, inside and out, ultimately, bringing the mega yacht back to Fort Lauderdale.

Our past projects had been big and rewarding on their own, but we both knew this was an enormous undertaking. I also knew that no captain ever gets this kind of opportunity. Mr. R. was once again giving me his valued trust in my abilities, but more importantly, he was giving me his unwavering faith in me as a person. My life was starting to come back full circle!

Stephanie and I had a lengthy conversation, and of course, in my excitement and enthusiasm, I realized it had become a one-sided conversation. Patiently and in her soft manner, she said, "Michael, do not worry about me, I'm able to take care of myself now. Of course, you have to go!" Sitting up in the bed she had spent so much time in these past months, she took my hand and said, "You deserve this, and I'm so very proud of you."

Within a week, I had found a new captain for the *Picante*. I made sure Steph had everything she needed. We also got news that the shooter's trial had been set for two months later. I assured the prosecutor I would be back for that!

Without having the time, I felt I needed to prepare, I was soon on the long trip to the small port town of Fremantle, Western Australia. After the twenty-four-hour trip, I was exhausted. But the intensity of my excitement at the start of this incredible adventure gave me an energy that surprised even myself.

I was met by the ship's captain, who along with his skeleton crew could not have been more friendly and accommodating. The yacht herself was a well-known mega yacht I had remembered seeing years ago in the South of France called *Sea Jewel*. It took five days and nights to assess her, looking through engine and maintenance logs, crawling through bilges, examining the ship's systems and mechanicals, and finally her hull integrity. I was now ready to make the call back to Mr. R.

Before that conversation, I had to process some thoughts. In our past projects, I had always tried to be truthful and succinct in my descriptions of the facts, good or bad, knowing there were millions of dollars at stake, depending on my report. But I also knew Mr. R. would put a lot of weight on my experience and personal feeling about this vessel. I decided to be somewhat understated in the good, pointing out the need for significant upgrades and the amount of money and time required, while also putting aside my huge desire for this incredible opportunity.

As always, his questions were few and informed. My general answers were, "Yes, *Sea Jewel* is very sound and solid, but she needs us."

The purchase was made. The logistics and organization were overwhelming, but I was confidant and knowledgeable on how to proceed.

One of the most important things to be done was to bring my first officer and friend, Lance, to help. He had served in the South African military. He was extremely loyal and had a habit of making me look like a far better captain than I actually was.

20

The Trial

We were soon well underway in *Sea Jewel's* renovation, and the date was coming up for the shooter's trial. As expected, I made the long trip back home, anxious to get this part of our lives behind us.

Stephanie and I arrived at the courthouse without much conversation. She was frightened and nervous, and I felt the same, but it was mixed with that anger that never seemed to be far away.

The two prosecutors met us inside the courtroom. Sitting on the other side was the shooter with his parents. The prosecutor proceeded to tell us that his lawyer wanted to make some sort of plea deal to keep him from going on trial and most likely avoid significant jail time.

"Absolutely not," I responded angrily. Steph put hand on my arm, calmly saying, "Let's hear what they have to say."

The prosecutor nodded, then said, "The father wants to come over and have a few words with you first."

Neither Stephanie nor I said anything as the prosecutor waved toward the other side of the room. I felt her hand squeeze mine as the father approached. He avoided my stare, not speaking for a few seconds. Finally, he said to Steph how terribly sorry he was this had happened. He reached inside his jacket and pulled out a picture of Stephanie, telling her that he had this on his refrigerator.

Before he could speak another word, I exploded out of my seat, coming within two inches from his face. The anger flooded my body. I spat out, "Your son is a punk-ass scumbag!"

Before I could say anything else, the father stumbled backward, tripping and falling. He scampered back to the other side of the court room. I felt the two prosecutors holding me while the deputies saw the commotion and hurried over.

Sitting back down next to Steph, shaking with anger, I felt her gently put her arm around my shoulders. Several minutes later, the prosecutor came back and said, "This is what they propose, he pleads guilty to a lesser felony, does two years' probation with no jail time and no trial, and will pay Stephanie $25,000 restitution." He continued, "This decision is yours; we are prepared to go to trial, but it's going to be ugly. I am also hesitant to put you on the stand, Michael. You will be an angry witness, and that's not good." I gave him a half smile and reluctantly agreed.

Stephanie's hand firmly turned my head to her, and with pleading, moist eyes, she said, "Please, Michael, I don't want a trial, please!"

Still looking at her, I could feel everyone else's stare. Pausing and trying to take this moment in, I caught myself firmly barking orders, "We will agree to no trial, but Stephanie and I want three years' probation. And you tell them he pays Stephanie $125,000 restitution. Take it or leave it!"

I slowly looked up at the prosecutors as they exchanged a look and headed over to the other side of the courtroom. Twenty minutes later, they came back and said they had agreed.

Stephanie and I quietly drove home. Not much was said, but we both felt a huge weight had been lifted. Later that evening, she called me into the bedroom. Lying there with a quiet, peaceful look, she just whispered, "Thank you."

I was booked to fly back to Australia in four days. The next three days were consumed with important meetings regarding the ship's business. My last night was spent organizing and laying things out for Stephanie, making sure she had what she needed because I was going to be away for many months. She was wonderful, pleasant, and we even shared some laughter. Both of us realized that we had not shared that experience in a very, very long time. In fact, It was good for both of us! But an unspoken sadness could also be felt. The experiences each of us had over the previous two years were completely different in their pain, yet very much the same. Knowing, but not knowing something had changed. So much that needed to be said but was not. Feelings that had to be expressed but were not. I flew out the next day.

The following few months were full of incredible challenges, unmoving obstacles, huge planning, and ultimately, consequential decision-making. I felt my focus and intensity kick up a few notches, which became clear when my first officer came to me and asked if he could give the crew a day off. I turned to face him, but before I could say anything, he said, "Captain, the crew has not had a day off in three months! They are exhausted! I need to give them a weekend away from the boat."

With a stunned look, I blurted out, "Oh my God! Of course, give them whatever time you think is necessary. I honestly did not realize. I'm sorry, Lance."

He looked at me with a knowing smile and said, "I know, Captain, I know."

I took a moment to realize what kind of pace I had been setting. My eighteen-hour days were draining the people around me. I was consumed by my own personal burden and the heavy weight of worry that I would miss any moment. Good or bad, I wanted to absorb all of it. I knew something had been given back to me, and I had never felt more alive.

The day finally came. Our sea trials were completed, and I felt confident in *Sea Jewel's* condition and ability to make the trip over halfway around the world. I had learned through the years that shipyards can become a sanctuary. I have seen some captains become prisoners to that shipyard, unable to separate what is essential to be done from what would be nice to be done. After six months of bringing *Sea Jewel* back to life, I set our departure date for one week.

I had spent several days plotting the 144 waypoints, charting our long trip. Our epic voyage was going to take us from Fremantle on the Indian Ocean, north around the northern territories of Australia, then through the Torres straits just south of Papua, New Guinea. We would then move down the east coast of Australia and through the Great Barrier Reef, stopping at Port Cairns, Australia for provisioning.

Heading east, our first stop before starting the long trip across the South Pacific would be Vanuatu. I planned a logistical stop in Fiji, then from there on to Tahiti. Moving across thousands of miles of open ocean, we would weave our way through the Tuamotus atolls and eventually meet our fuel barge on the island of Nuka Hiva in the Marquesas Islands, French Polynesia.

From there, we would cross another long stretch of open ocean, crossing the equator heading toward Galapagos and up to the Panama Canal. Finally, we would make our last long run north through the western Caribbean and home to Fort Lauderdale.

I knew what was ahead of us, but I needed to have a few words with the crew.

We now had a total of twelve crew members, mostly young and unproven deck hands, interior crew, and of course the experienced engineers and first officer I depended on completely.

We gathered downstairs in the crew mess. I started by thanking them for their dedication and hard work these past months, then told them about our departure plans and schedule.

For our newer crew, I relayed briefly the long, difficult, and sometimes dangerous days ahead. I told them it was essential that they perform their duties to the tee. No cutting corners, no matter how small it might seem, because our lives might depend on it.

I continued, "You have all gone through our emergency drills and protocols. Remember your training and the things that have been taught you. Embrace that knowledge. It will give you confidence when needed." Pausing, I said, "Now for the good stuff. What you are about to be a part of, without a doubt, will be life-changing for all of you. You will go places, experience things, that very few people ever have. You will witness nature at its meanest, but also at its most remarkable! But most important, I can guarantee that you will learn who you really are.

"Grasp the magnitude of this experience and accomplishment. I promise you; the satisfaction of your achievement will be monumental in defining who you become and know that it will stay with you the rest of your life."

One more thing of importance had to be said. I told them I understood that for the next several months, their lives will be directly affected on a daily basis, and their safety and well-being will depend solely on my decision-making. I take that responsibility very seriously and promised that I would not let them down, finally thanking them for their trust.

21

The Voyage

"Half my life was spent in a ship's cabin.
But my front yard was the world's oceans."

Sea Jewel left the small port of Fremantle to fanfare and cheers. All of us expressed gratitude and said good-bye to the wonderful people who had been so generous with their help and friendship, making this town feel like home. I knew I would miss this place.

Our journey turned out to be far more than any of us had imagined. Making the long run up the west coast of Australia, we turned east, coming around the vast deep fjords of the northern territories. We were hit with strong winds and rough seas. Deciding to get out of weather, I plotted a course down inside one of these carved out trenches of water. Slowly making our way deep inside one, I took in the incredible empty vastness on both sides. It was a legendary no-man's-land that you could easily imagine on an alien planet.

Lance, standing outside on the wheelhouse wing, spotted an airplane. Suddenly the VHF radio crackled to life. A man with a thick Aussie accent stated directly, "Hey, mate, Australian Coast Guard here. You down there in the big white boat, it is extremely rare seeing anyone up this way. Who are you, and where are you headed?"

Lance stepped inside. We looked at each other, puzzled but thrilled to hear from someone. I picked up the VHF and calmly gave him a pleasant good day, identifying myself as captain of the *Sea Jewel*. I gave him the ship's call sign and port of registry, then told him Fremantle was our port of debarkation and we were headed toward Darwin for fuel, then down to Cairns and ultimately across the Pacific to America.

We heard him give a low whistle over the speaker, then he said, "Well, Captain, we heard you boys were headed this way and I have a couple of things you need to pay attention to." He warned me to find deep water before I dropped the hook, otherwise I would be high and dry in morning. I knew the tides were some of the most dramatic in world up here, but until you see it for yourself, you are never quite prepared for the drastic change in sea levels in this place.

But his last piece of advice was given in a deadly serious tone that I have never forgotten: "One more thing, mate. Whatever you do, do not let anyone go ashore. Don't even let your crew go anywhere near water level."

He got his point across, briefly telling me that a sailboat had come by this way last year. The captain's wife and a crew member took their dingy ashore to take pictures. The captain watched from his deck as an enormous saltwater croc came out of the water. The giant prehistoric monster chased down his wife and ate her in front of his eyes! Listening in stunned astonishment, Lance and I looked at each other, our mouths wide open. With a pause for effect, he happily wished us a good and safe voyage. With that, they were gone.

Weeks passed, and our trip had already given us so much to overcome, but also immense joy. After the sometimes terror-filled experience of climbing huge mountains of water over hundreds of miles of open ocean, we relished the time we spent in a few magnificent tropical paradises, along with the generous hospitality of the wonderful island locals. But then one of the most majestic and wondrous things I had ever witnessed at sea happened.

On this calm quiet morning, only the noise of the low constant drone of our engines could be heard. With ships binoculars and keeping my routine, I was scanning out over the vast empty ocean. Suddenly, the sensation that instinct gives you, made my hands tighten and my focus narrow. Fifteen to twenty miles away, a rumbling and immense churning of water spread across the horizon I could see it before hearing it. A tsunami of erupting water as far as you could see, was coming right at us.

Staring intently through the binoculars, I whispered, "Oh my God!" I had seen these natural phenomena before, but nothing even close to this magnitude. I yelled to my deckhand, "Go below! Get everyone on deck, everyone now!" Startled and looking a little frightened, he darted downstairs.

From miles and miles away, the dolphins heard the hum of our engines and came in masse to greet us on a scale that was unimaginable. Jumping, leaping, and with high-pitched chatter, they surrounded and raced by the ship. They were so close we could almost reach and out touch them. Concerned, I quickly backed down our engines. The noise was deafening. As far as we could see, thousands and thousands and thousands of dolphins kept on coming.

This magnificent spectacle lasted over three hours, leaving the entire crew awestruck and screaming with laughter, with many of us in tears. Afterward, we felt drained but knew we had just witnessed an event that would be impossible to describe. With smiles all around, I could feel a distinct lift in crew morale. As captain, after so long at sea, that is always welcome. I knew some of the crew had just experienced one of those life-changing events.

Weeks later, finally leaving one of the most incredible places I had ever visited, the island of Nuka Hiva in the Marquesas, we were headed northeast toward the equator. It was a flat, calm, steamy hot, crystal clear day when the ship's satellite phone rang, startling me and the deckhand on watch.

Thinking it was Mr. R., I was anxious to tell him of our progress. Instead, there was a short silence, and then I heard Stephanie's voice saying, "Michael?"

I could tell by her tone that it was serious. "Steph?" I asked with nervous hesitation, "Are you okay?"

Once again, it was one of those moments when a person knows what is coming without knowing. In what I could tell was a somewhat rehearsed dialogue, she told me she was leaving. She said she was so very sorry to tell me this way but was unable to wait until I got home. Not really sounding like Stephanie, she said, "It was the only way I could do this."

Finally, with an internal kind of shrug and sigh, I replied, "I understand, please take whatever you need. Just make sure you're okay."

Being difficult to have any kind of conversation over ships satellite phone, that is all I managed to say. Hanging up, it was not a hurt I felt inside. I had expected this outcome, and I felt a deeper resolve to complete what I had committed to finishing.

Our Ship's heading was set for our next waypoint the Galapagos islands, Ecuador. I had arranged a fuel stop months beforehand which required an enormous amount of paperwork and permitting. We were very close to the equator, and I wanted to keep a close eye on our satellite GPS position. I planned on stopping the vessel and gather the crew for a toast and rite of passage upon crossing the equator. This was an old tradition amongst sailors who have had the opportunity to make such a passage.

Being at the equator, the days were clear and hot. About two hundred miles out of the islands we knew we were getting close as evidenced by the abundance of birds starting to circle the ship. But these were not ordinary sea gulls or any other kind of birds that I had ever seen. Against the backdrop of the pristine clear blue sky, their all black color and enormous size made them appear truly prehistoric. For miles we watched them circle our ship in a somewhat menacing manner like something right out of Jurassic Park.

Arriving in the Galapagos, we were directed to tie up alongside an old fuel dock in a somewhat isolated area. The permits that were granted Sea Jewel, only allowed us to stay two days. We set to work taking on a few thousand gallons of fuel knowing it would take one entire day and well into the night to complete. Almost immediately after docking, two enormous sea lions got up onto our aft deck's lower platform at water level and promptly made themselves at home. The curiosity and wonder they provided us was priceless.

We were well under way with our fueling procedures, as I stood on the dock watching and making sure our safety protocols were followed. I concluded my conversation with a few locals and made my way down the dock to see how our two sea lion guests were doing on the swim platform.

The Sun was starting to set. I stood with arms crossed, looking around, taking in the remote and magnificent beauty of these unusual and captivating islands. As my mind drifted, I caught myself thinking about where I was and what I was doing. Just eighteen months earlier I was fighting to survive the despicable and degrading existence of a faraway foreign prison. At that moment I think I knew the demons of those prisons were going to follow me for a long time. But if there was such a thing as divine redemption, I was living it.

Deep in thought, I felt a gentle touch on my arm. Startled I turned to face one of our young stewardesses. A bright and pretty young woman we had hired back in Fremantle. She asked with slight concern, "Captain, are you OK?" "Of course, of course," I replied.

She stood next to me for a few minutes, not saying anything as we watched our enormous guests on the back of the boat, both of us enjoying their contentment. Staring straight ahead, she quietly stated, "Thank You Captain." Then turned and headed back down the dock.

I watched her walk away and smiled to myself, thinking not long ago she had never so much as crossed a small lake in a boat.

And having the courage to be a part of something she knew nothing about, she took that chance on adventure. Coming out on the other side, a strong and capable young person. Yes, absolutely, divine redemption I thought.

We left the Galapagos with a bit of regret at not being able to stay longer. But in our short time it did provide a unique and unforgettable experience. Heading northeast towards the Panama Canal, I was able to reach our ships agent by long range SSB (single side band radio) once we got into range. We were told to drop anchor on the Pacific side of the canal and wait for our turn in line. Huge cargo ships and others were before us and only so many can fit inside the locks. After three days we were called. With the Panamanian Pilot onboard, we made the spectacular trip through the locks of the Panama Canal to the other side and into Gatun Lake. Weaving and navigating our way through the water ways cut out of the thick jungles, we finally arrived at the Balboa side of the canal and into the Caribbean Sea.

I took a moment to reflect on my last trip through the canal. A few years earlier and what seemed like several lifetimes ago, I had brought the Picante down from San Diego through the canal on her maiden voyage to Fort Lauderdale for Mr.R. Since that time, I have always thought the Panama Canal experience is something extremely special. This trip was no less memorable.

We were on our last and final leg of our passage over halfway around the world. Headed north to Florida.

On New Year's Eve day, 1999, I pulled *Sea Jewel* alongside the dock in Fort Lauderdale. We had made it! Over thirteen thousand miles at sea. Including stops along the way, our voyage had taken over four months.

After many greetings and completing the ship's duties, the day was winding down. I sat alone up top in the wheelhouse. Calling down to the crews' mess, I asked Lance (my 1st officer) if he would come up for a minute to see me. He quietly climbed the stairs, and

I asked him to sit. We smiled at each other, both feeling that deep satisfaction of accomplishment. We had sailed together many years and across thousands of miles of open ocean. I came to know the character of this man like no other.

"Thank you, my dear friend," I said in a tone that needed no interpretation.

"No, Captain, thank you, well done, sir," he replied in his precise military tone.

Silently nodding and meeting his stare, I told him with my eyes and a quick smile how much he meant to me as an officer, shipmate, and most importantly my friend. Finally, I said, "Tell the crew I will stay onboard tonight and do the ship's watch. I want all of them to go ashore, enjoy themselves, and give them the day off tomorrow."

He gave me a big smile and started back down the stairs. Then he turned and said, "In an hour, Captain, the crew would like you to come downstairs. "

An hour later, I walked into the crew's area. Everyone had seated themselves around the huge mess table. In the center was a cake our chef had baked.

All was quiet as I read what had been written on the enormous cake: "Captain, we will sail with you anywhere."

A simple sentence that said it all. Feeling the emotion flood the room, I slowly looked up with moist eyes, giving each crew member a knowing smile and a single nod of respect.

The pendulum had truly swung back my way.

Sea Jewel was a magnificent world cruiser. Giving us great adventures.

Sea Jewel crew. Great crew and even better people.

Michael with *Sea Jewel*, Fremantle, W. Australia.

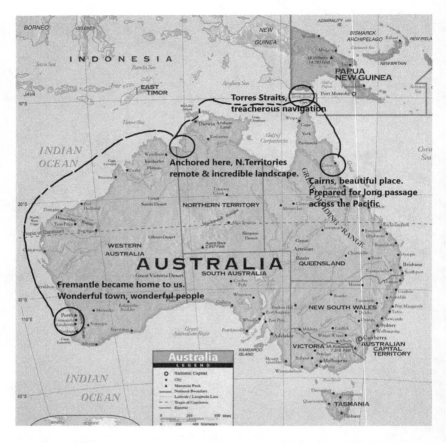

Sea Jewel's passage around Australia. Our stops are noted on the map.

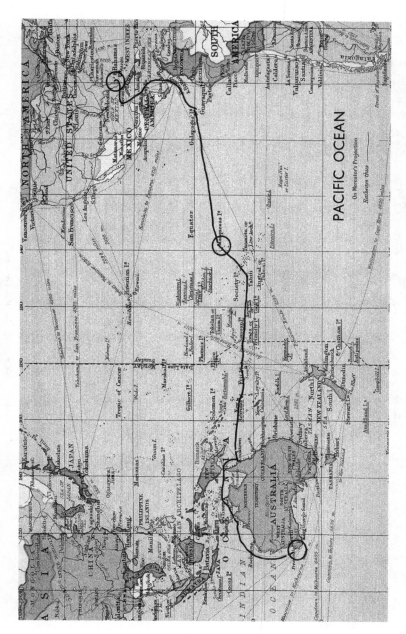

The voyage of *Sea Jewel* became the longest private yacht delivery on record. Over 13,000 miles at sea.

Bora Bora, South Pacific.

The island of Nuka Hiva, Marquesas, French Polynesia. The island beauty was spectacular. The people were more so. Truly a magical place.

Ancient stone carving on Nuka Hiva.

Epilogue

The next couple of years seemed like a blur. I continued working for Mr. R. More projects, more voyages, but nothing quite like the *Sea Jewel*.

That trip became huge yachting news, prompting invitations from boating publications for interviews and speaking engagements. Many captains contacted me, asking for information on how I planned such a long trip and how to find the ships' agents and local help required for that kind of undertaking. It opened the door for other owners to send their vessels to these remote and adventurous destinations.

Two years passed, and I had not seen or spoken with Stephanie since that short conversation we had in the middle of the Pacific Ocean.

On one particular night, a captain friend asked me to go with him to a huge fundraising event the yachting community was putting on.

I usually avoided large gatherings like this, but he was unusually persuasive. We arrived at a huge outside venue, where a couple hundred people were listening to loud music, a bar had been set up, and a stage had been built for speeches and awards. I found a comfortable place to stand, greeting familiar people who stopped to say hello.

Suddenly, I felt something. Reacting to that feeling of someone staring at me. I slowly turned around. Searching across the packed area of people, I saw her. Seated on a platform, looking right at me with a warm beautiful smile, was Stephanie. I felt paralyzed by the butterflies in my stomach. Slowly making my way toward her, neither of us taking our eyes away, I felt myself smiling. She came down the few steps and stood close, right in front of me.

She said kindly, in her familiar voice, "Michael, "How are you?" The wave of emotion was immense! I managed to say, "I'm fine." Finding my voice, I continued, "You look great."

She lifted her once-crippled leg and asked, "What do you think, looking better?"

We were sharing warm affectionate smiles. Finally, in a rush to get it out, I said, "Stephanie, there is so much I've wanted to say to you. Most of all, to thank you for everything you did for me. I never asked what you needed or wanted. I realized it was you who was always there, following what I wanted to do. I'm so, so sorry."

Taking my hands and looking up with tear-filled eyes, she softly replied, "Michael, I made mistakes I'll have to live with the rest of my life. For many years, you gave me a life that was incredible. But most of all, you taught me how to be so much more than I thought I could ever be. For that I will always love you."

She paused, then went on, "I had to leave, Michael. If I had stayed, it would only have caused more damage. I couldn't help you anymore, we were both so broken, and I realized we could not fix each other."

Some people nearby called to her and she turned. "Don't go yet," I pleaded. Thinking, but not telling her, there is so much I need to say, so much I am sorry for. "I have to, this is my event. I'm the organizer," she answered. Still smiling, I gave her a proud nod and said, "Of course it is."

She turned to go, but after a few steps she stopped. Looking back through her once-familiar, beautiful, tear-filled green eyes, I heard her say above the loud music and crowd, "Michael, you will always be my captain."

With a deep sigh, I felt that vicious vice called heartache, grip, and start to squeeze my fragile psyche. I felt my protective shell begin to crack. Suddenly, not being able to breath, I gasped for air.

Watching her surrounded by friends, disappearing into the mass of people, she was gone.

My brothers and sisters Oct. 2019. They are my Life!!!!

My beloved dog, Jack. He knew I needed him before I did. A great great friend, I miss him every day. RIP

Michael with family and their beloved Aunt Carmen.

Michael is retired but still lives and enjoys life on the ocean.

Michael with his sister Doris and twin sister Michelle.

About the Author

Captain Churchward has been the subject of an *MSNBC Dateline* special program and several human-interest stories and has been featured in numerous yacht publications. He is now retired and enjoying life in South Florida.

CPSIA information can be obtained
at www.ICGtesting.com
Printed in the USA
LVHW091136171120
671902LV00007B/143